ELIZABETH I

Geoffrey Regan

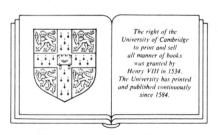

The right of the
University of Cambridge
to print and sell
all manner of books
was granted by
Henry VIII in 1534.
The University has printed
and published continuously
since 1584.

CAMBRIDGE UNIVERSITY PRESS

Cambridge
New York   Port Chester
Melbourne   Sydney

Published by the Press Syndicate of the University of Cambridge
The Pitt Building, Trumpington Street, Cambridge CB2 1RP
32 East 57th Street, New York, NY 10022, USA
10 Stamford Road, Oakleigh, Melbourne 3166, Australia

First published 1988
Reprinted 1989

Printed in Great Britain at the University Press, Cambridge

British Library cataloguing in publication data

Regan, Geoffrey
    Elizabeth I. – (Cambridge topics in
    history).
    1. Great Britain – History – Elizabeth,
    1558–1603
    I. Title
    942.05'5   DA355

Library of Congress cataloguing in publication data

Regan, Geoffrey.
    Elizabeth I.
    (Cambridge topics in history)
    Bibliography. ;·
    Includes index.
    1. Great Britain – History – Elizabeth, 1558–1603.
2. Elizabeth I, Queen of England, 1558–1603.   I. Title.
II. Series.
DA355.R43   1987   941.085   87-22414

ISBN 0 521 31291 4

SE

Acknowledgements

The author and publisher would like to thank the following for permission to reproduce extracts:

p. 17, Acts of the Privy Council, 1589, PRO ref. 0106 PC2/16, vol. 17, pp. 413–5, Crown copyright material in the Public Record Office is reproduced by permission of the Controller of Her Majesty's Stationery Office; 2.2 J. Neale, *Elizabeth and her Parliaments*, Johathan Cape; 2.19 and 2.21 C. Read, *Lord Burghley and Queen Elizabeth*, Jonathan Cape; J. Lynch, *Spain under the Habsburgs*, Basil Blackwell; 4.11 *The Execution of Justice*, ed. R. Kingdom, Folger Shakespeare Library; 5.8 and 6.11 *William Lambarde and Local Government*, ed. C. Read, Folger Shakespeare Library

Cover illustration: sketch for a miniature of Elizabeth I by Isaac Oliver, *c.*1592, Victoria & Albert Museum

Contents

To John Crook, with thanks . . .

Introduction

It is sometimes necessary for historians to liberate historical figures from the image-makers of their own times and this is certainly so in the case of Elizabeth I. She ascended the throne of England at a time of religious and political upheaval in Europe. As the living symbol of Henry VIII's original break with Rome she was hailed as the saviour of Protestantism in England, as well as God's bulwark in Europe against the Catholic Antichrist. The problem was that Elizabeth did not necessarily see things this way. In fact, for much of her reign there was to be a clash between the cautious and conservative queen and the image that her loyal Protestant advisers had of her.

Most of the crucial issues of her reign, such as the Succession, the treatment of Mary Stuart, the intervention in the Netherlands and the reform of the Church, involved Elizabeth in trying to avoid the consequences of the very image used to make her rule legitimate. However, she was the Protestants' only hope and, unpalatable as their support for her often was, she could not survive without it.

Elizabeth's early life undoubtedly had a profound effect on how she acted as Queen. Declared a bastard at the age of three, and constantly reminded of it by militant Catholics, she had to endure the difficulties of an orphan upbringing and, at an impressionable age, the attentions of the handsome but irresponsible Thomas Seymour. It is possible that these early events scarred her psychologically and perhaps this helps to explain her attitude towards marriage. Her education, under the great humanist scholar Roger Ascham, formed a serious and learned young woman, who could speak French and Italian fluently. During her sister Mary's reign, she carefully avoided being drawn into plots planned on her behalf and became politically astute beyond her years.

She came to the throne at the age of twenty-five, Protestant in religion yet no radical, conservative in politics, grounded in a humanist education and the traditions of English kingship and believing above all that she took her authority from God and from no man. She was concerned to maintain the status quo where possible. In religious affairs she knew that changes would have to take place, but these were changes which would carry the stamp of law and the approval of Parliament.

In 1558, she was faced with problems which were to dominate her reign. It was an achievement merely to keep these at arm's length, even if she never solved them all. As a woman in a world dominated by men, she was to be constantly reminded of her duty to marry and secure the succession. Furthermore, the clash of religious views within the country was to remain a constant threat [1.1]. In foreign affairs she inherited a disastrous war with France, which had already cost the country Calais, England's last possession on the continent. She needed to maintain the friendship of Philip II of Spain to counter the threat from the Franco-Scottish union. Another recurring theme was the problem of government finance in the face of inflation and escalating costs from foreign wars. To strengthen her position she was forced to increase demands on local government, often at a cost resented by the gentry, who were accustomed to low taxation. The combined effects of wars, poor harvests and inflation, brought about such suffering among the poor that the stability of social order was threatened. Nevertheless, in encouraging local efforts to curb the effects of poverty, Elizabeth's government was initiating a programme of poor relief that would last until the nineteenth century.

The Settlement of 1559

On the death of Queen Mary, negotiations at Cateau Cambresis to end the war with France were halted, and English representatives returned home for fresh instructions. Elizabeth was immediately faced with financial and military problems and expected at any time to have to resist an invasion from Scotland. In creating her Privy Council, she reduced its members from thirty-nine to a more managable nineteen, retaining ten of her sister's councillors. The Marquis of Winchester, for instance, continued as Lord Treasurer. Of the new members, William Cecil was to play a prominent part in advising the new Queen in his capacity as Secretary of State.

Elizabeth's Council was to be the basis of her government: a strong team at whose centre was an inner circle connected to the Queen by ties of blood or friendship. As the reign progressed these men increased their power on the Council at the expense of the great magnates. In 1558, however, the new Council faced immediate problems: securing peace with France and Scotland, and achieving a settlement of religion which would bind the country together after the divisions of the last three reigns.

The religious settlement of 1559 has been the subject of recent historical dispute. In 1950 the great historian of Elizabeth's parliaments, J. Neale, argued that by introducing a Protestant Prayer Book, Elizabeth did not wish to establish a thoroughly Protestant Church but wanted to restore the Royal Supremacy, consigning the form of worship to a later meeting of Convocation. Neale asserted that the Acts of Supremacy and Uniformity, which emerged after the Easter parliamentary recess, were signs that the

Queen had suffered defeat at the hands of radical Protestants in the House of Commons. She was forced to depend on Marian exiles as her bishops, because the existing bishops had refused to accept her supremacy in the Church.

However, N. L. Jones has recently claimed that the Settlement which emerged in 1559 was the one that Elizabeth actually wanted. The bill proposed in the Lower House to introduce the 1552 Prayer Book was decisively defeated in the House of Lords, where the resistance of Marian bishops had been underestimated by Elizabeth's advisers [1.8 and 1.9]. Faced with the possible defeat of her proposals, Elizabeth decided to reconvene Parliament after the Easter recess, as much parliamentary time had been taken up with bills for the restitution of church lands. During the recess, two bishops were arrested and imprisoned in the Tower, thus weakening the capacity of Catholic peers to obstruct the Settlement in the Upper House. The outcome was an easy passage for the Act of Supremacy, but the Act of Uniformity passed by just three votes in a hostile House of Lords. In Jones's view, the Settlement was a triumph for both the Queen and the Commons.

Historians are by no means united in accepting this interpretation, for it calls into question much of Neale's work on the part played by radical Protestants in Parliament during the 1560s. However, in support of Jones, it can be argued that the Settlement seems closest to what we know of Elizabeth's own religious views [1.3].

The Act of Supremacy (1559) involved a compromise. As a concession to both ardent Catholics and Protestant zealots, neither of which groups could accept a lay person – especially a woman – as Head of the Church, Elizabeth took the title of 'Supreme Governor' [1.7]. This was clearly intended to emphasise the Queen's essentially lay role, in contrast with that of her father, who would have considered himself of semi-ecclesiastical rank. How much Elizabeth felt inhibited by this is open to debate.

The Act of Uniformity (1559) also showed the Queen's intention to create a Church in which as many believers as possible could find salvation [1.12]. Though the 1552 Prayer Book was to be used, the wording from the 1549 Prayer Book was to be incorporated in the Communion service, to allow an interpretation involving the Real Presence. On a second point the Radicals were to encounter difficulty with Elizabeth's own interpretation of Church ritual [1.13 and 1.14]. The use of vestments, as authorised in 1549, was to result in major controversy during the 1560s and eventually lead to a breakaway movement by the Nonconformists.

The Succession and foreign policy

Elizabeth played a prominent part in foreign policy which, for the first twenty-five years of her reign, was tied up with questions of her marriage and the succession to the throne. While her Councillors, particularly Cecil and later Walsingham, might take the lead in developing lines of policy, she retained the ultimate responsibility and did not hesitate to spurn their advice. In the early years of the reign there was a likelihood that when she did marry, her husband's own religious views might lead to a revision, if not a complete reversal of the Settlement of 1559. In spite of this, the main fear on the part of her advisers was that she would die without an heir and plunge the country into the confusion of a disputed succession. Unless she could be persuaded to name her heir or marry and produce one herself no one could rest secure. However, the uncertainty of her life as heir to her sister, Mary, had shown Elizabeth the dangers a ruler might face from revolts on behalf of the next-in-succession.

How serious her intention to marry was, is open to doubt. Protracted negotiations for marriage to the Archdukes Ferdinand or Charles contented Spain after she had rejected Philip II's suit, yet never seemed likely to succeed. It was not until she had passed the age of child-bearing that, in her relationship with Francis, Duke of Alençon, she revealed her profoundly emotional nature. It seems possible that her early experiences scarred her capacity to form human relationships, a problem exacerbated by her view of herself as a queen married to her kingdom, and by memories of her sister's disastrous marriage.

In spite of her unwillingness to acknowledge Mary, Queen of Scots as her heir [2.3], in her heart she must have known that without a child of her own, Mary Stuart might well succeed her. Legitimist as she was, Elizabeth found it difficult to know how to treat her fellow sovereign [2.4]. The mere presence of Mary in England after 1568 created the very dangers of which she had warned Parliament. The successive failures of the Ridolfi, Throckmorton and Babington Plots says much for the loyalty and efficiency of Elizabeth's servants.

Elizabeth's relations with Mary Stuart were a curious mixture of personal and public reactions on the part of the English Queen. As a believer in the Divine Right of monarchs, she felt it necessary to show her 'sister' all the respect due to her position. In spite of all the evidence provided for her by Walsingham and his spies, she found the idea of 'public' justice in the shape of execution almost impossible to accept. However, when she found that she could not pass on this unenviable burden, she relieved her own guilt both publicly and privately by using Secretary Davison as a scapegoat. The eventual peaceful accession of James VI in 1603 owed little to Elizabeth, who had refused to name her successor, but was the result of the skilful diplomacy of Robert Cecil.

There has been academic dispute about how much 'policy' was to be found in Elizabeth's foreign policy, particularly towards Spain and the Netherlands. R. B. Wernham believes that Elizabeth had a clear course but followed a track full of twists and turns, responding on a day-to-day basis to the actions of other states. On the question of the Netherlands her purposes were clearly the restoration of ancient liberties and home rule for the Netherlands, the removal of a Spanish army which could threaten English interests, and the prevention of French expansion there. It was a policy based on a fear of France as much as of Spain. Wernham considers this policy far-sighted and successful.

However, C. Wilson's view differs and he describes Elizabeth's policy as based on a succession of expedients, culminating in failure. Recently W. T. MacCaffrey has detected some consistent principles in her foreign policy, similar to those proposed by Wernham. However, he sees Elizabeth as a reactor to events rather than an initiator, being forced by the ebb-and-flow of events to improvise.

English foreign trade had for long been linked with the great port of Antwerp, through which it entered Europe. This had dictated the need for friendship with the House of Burgundy and, by 1558, this meant the King of Spain. Elizabeth's dependence on revenue from an export tax on woollen cloth sent to Antwerp by the Merchant Adventurers, meant that this trade was vital to her. However, the relationship with Spain was fragile and was to be shattered in 1568 by the incompetence of the new Spanish ambassador to England, Don Guerau de Spes. De Spes was by no means an able diplomat and had little experience of, or love for, the English. His reports to King Philip of the members of the Queen's Council were particularly misleading and only tended to sour relations further [**2.9 and 2.10**]. He also informed Philip that Elizabeth's economic problems were so severe that a further trade embargo would cause her to return to Catholicism. This was absolutely incorrect. Nevertheless, Elizabeth was always looking for the opportunity to borrow money at lower rates of interest than were common on the Antwerp bourse. Thus, in November 1568, when Spanish ships carrying Italian gold to pay Alva's soldiers in the Netherlands were forced by bad weather and French pirates to take shelter in an English harbour, Elizabeth sought to appropriate it for her own use. But de Spes, realising that the gold would be seized, advised Alva in the Netherlands to arrest English merchants and their goods [**2.10**]. This was a grave miscalculation and provoked a crisis which neither Philip nor Elizabeth had sought.

The break with Spain was inevitable. Neither Philip nor Elizabeth were free agents and both were later thrust into crusading postures in which neither was comfortable. English mariners, led by John Hawkins and the young Francis Drake, were already breaking into Spanish waters in search of trade or plunder. In fact, news of the Spanish attack on Hawkins at San Juan de Ulloa had reached England shortly before Elizabeth's seizure of the gold and may have contributed to that action.

The Papal Bull issued in 1570 **[4.9]** condemned Elizabeth as a heretic, and released her people from allegiance to her. Henceforth there could be no peace between Elizabeth and the Papal See. In 1572 the new pope, Gregory XIII, declared that the destruction of Elizabeth and all her works was the master purpose of his life.

Although during the 1570s there was a rapprochement with Spain it could not be sustained. The revolt of the Netherlands took on a more desperate character after 1576 and Elizabeth was hard pressed to resist pressure from her own Council to intervene militarily. However, she was still content to play an indirect role, until the death of the Duke of Anjou (Alençon) and the assassination of William of Orange in 1584 seemed to anticipate a complete victory for Spain. Moreover, the growth of the Catholic League in France threatened to create an anti-English union which controlled the entire southern coastline of the Channel. It was for this that she signed the Treaty of Nonsuch in 1585 with the United Provinces, and agreed to send Leicester with troops to help the Dutch rebels **[2.15]**. Elizabeth's support for Protestants in France and the Netherlands was less a product of religious conviction than of political expediency. Surrounded as she was by Protestant advisers, pressing her to intervene as the champion of her religion, she resisted such siren cries because she hated war and its cost in men and treasure **[2.14 and 2.16]**.

In 1559 Elizabeth had been forced to accept the loss of Calais, though she concealed the fact as long as possible, by a legalistic fiction contained in the Treaty of Cateau Cambresis. Nevertheless, though peace with France had removed one threat, another loomed large. Three months after the treaty was signed, Francis II, husband of Mary, Queen of Scots, became King of France. Mary Stuart, as a grand-daughter of Margaret Tudor, had a plausible claim to the English throne, and promptly added the title of Queen of England to her string – an action much resented by Elizabeth. However, a Protestant-inspired rebellion in Scotland, supported by the English, succeeded in ridding the country of French influence and overthrowing papal supremacy there. Thus when Francis II died and the young Mary Stuart returned to her homeland she found the situation much changed.

After the failure of the expedition to Le Havre in 1562 Elizabeth maintained peaceful relations with France throughout the rest of the decade. The rift with Spain led to a diplomatic re-alignment with France and the idea was proposed of a marriage between Elizabeth and one of the sons of Catherine de Medici. In spite of the absurd disparity in ages between Elizabeth and the young Alençon, and the decreasing likelihood that the marriage would be fruitful, the negotiations continued for over a decade. During this period Elizabeth acquired an influence in French politics which, after the massacre of St Bartholomew's Day in 1572, led to her strong support for Henry of Navarre as the legitimate claimant to the throne. By 1576 Elizabeth was also lending money to the rebels in the Netherlands in their struggle against Spain, though she had no love of rebels, particularly Calvinist ones. The breakdown in the marriage negotiations with Alençon (later Duke of Anjou) resulted from domestic discontent with the idea of a marriage to a Catholic prince – and a French one at that! Nevertheless, Elizabeth supported Anjou's abortive campaigns in the Netherlands to help the rebels there.

Elizabeth has often been called parsimonious in financing the war against Spain, yet her aims were defensive, not offensive. She had none of her father's love of military splendour *per se*, and was suspicious of military adventures. She desired no further territory than she had inherited; but against rebellion within – as in Ireland – she was ruthless.

Foreign wars were financed by Crown revenue and supplemented by parliamentary subsidies. It is estimated that the war in the Netherlands cost Elizabeth in excess of £2 million while the conquest of Ireland cost even more. If one adds to that the extensive naval activities and the various amphibious expeditions of the decade following the Armada, the difficulties she faced in financing them all become apparent.

According to historian R. B. Wernham, after 1594 England began to withdraw from continental war, except in the Netherlands, and began to concentrate on commercial war at sea. Where Elizabeth's foreign policy had been concerned with a European scenario, namely to prevent Spanish domination of the Netherlands and northern France, the emphasis changed to a war for the domination of the Atlantic ocean and maritime supremacy. Combined with this was the desire to prevent western Europe being dominated by any single power. However, the burden of the fighting on the continent, and in Ireland too after 1595, combined with natural disasters like bad harvests to impose a crippling burden on Elizabeth's realm at the end of her reign. The war brought few successes like the 1596 Cadiz expedition, and criticism of central government and even the monarch herself became widespread.

The Church of England and the Puritans

The Church in 1559 lacked many things, not least a uniform doctrine and committed clergy. The Settlement of 1559 had been established by Parliament, but it would take many years before it could be fully implemented at local level. The clergy who had sworn the Oath of Supremacy to Elizabeth as Supreme Governor of the Church were not a unified force: many had conformed simply to keep their livings and few were whole-hearted supporters of the new ways.

The publication of the Thirty Nine Articles in 1563 provided a doctrinal basis for the Church. The royal injunctions of 1559 [3.6] laid down minimum standards to be expected of clergy and bishops alike – although these standards were often not met [3.7]. In response to criticism from Catholic theologians that the new Church was merely the product of political expediency, Anglican thinkers like Bishop Jewel of Salisbury emphasised the new church's links with the early Christian Church and its biblical purity.

Mary's bishops had, with the exception of the Bishop of Llandaff, refused to serve under Elizabeth and the new Queen lost the services of many able clergy. Although she had done her best to accommodate moderate Catholics within the reformed Church, it had proved impossible. As a result she was forced to appoint some of the Marian exiles, people without episcopal experience and frequently strongly influenced by German or Swiss reformers. The new Archbishop of Canterbury, Matthew Parker, was one of the few who had stayed in England during Mary's persecutions. Some of the bishops Elizabeth chose, like Bishop Grindal of London, laid great stress on the importance of preaching and on the education of a clergy. He saw his role as a pastoral one, whereas Elizabeth emphasised its disciplinary purpose.

On the death of Archbishop Parker in 1575, Elizabeth chose Grindal to replace him. However, within a year they were to clash on the issue of 'Prophesyings'. Grindal believed them to be essential to improving standards among the clergy, but Elizabeth saw them as potentially subversive of the Royal Supremacy. Grindal's refusal to suppress them and his reprimand to the Queen [3.10] were unprecedented [3.11]. The suspension of Grindal and the gradual replacement through age and death of the first generation of her bishops by people more to her liking were indicative of the firm hold that Elizabeth intended to keep on her Church. Her choice of John Whitgift as Archbishop after Grindal's death, showed that she intended to show no leniency towards Nonconformists.

Many of the lower clergy were survivors of one or even two national changes in religion. Less than 300 of the 9,000 clergymen refused the Oath of Supremacy and chose to give up their livings, though probably a large number were conformist in name only. However, the poor quality and inadequate training of the lower clergy presented an even greater problem than sheer lack of numbers. The requirement that preachers possess a degree of Master of Arts was far too high, and many parishes were deprived of sermons, having to make do with the reading of homilies. The Puritan ideal of a preacher for every parish was far from being achieved in Elizabeth's reign. The Queen and the bishops she chose in the second half of her reign were emphatically hierarchical in their view of the Church. They resented the influence of the itinerant preacher or lecturer, usually a person of Puritan sympathies, who acted outside normal ecclesiastical channels.

The Act of Uniformity had imposed a fine of twelve pence for non-attendance at church, though to what extent this was strictly applied is open to debate. The onus was on local churchwardens and there were many examples in this period of their shortcomings. Although the original intention had been to force Catholics into the new Church, this aim was naive. Many conformed to avoid the fine, only to hear mass later elsewhere.

For many, the counter-attractions on Sundays – such as dancing, village games and the ale-house – made lengthy sermons or homilies unappealing [3.8 and 3.9]. Catechism classes – teaching through sets of questions – were one way of educating the poor in religion, and Elizabeth's reign witnessed the publication of over a hundred different catechisms. Parents were supposed to instruct their children and servants at home, while the clergy would hold classes for the poor and ignorant on Sundays.

Those who had returned to England from Switzerland and Germany in 1558, like bishops John Jewel and Edwin Sandys, had maintained firm links with the Protestant reformers they had met there. When facing a difficult doctrinal point they frequently sought advice from abroad. From 1559 onwards, the advice given by reformers like Peter Martyr and Bullinger takes increasing note of the political realities of the English situation [3.1]. They advised Jewel, Sandys and others to come to terms with Elizabeth's aims and aspirations and not to leave the Church, even if this meant compromising on issues such as the wearing of vestments. It was clear that those Radicals who would not reach an accommodation on these things 'indifferent' could not remain within the new Church.

The term 'Puritan' is particularly difficult to apply accurately in this period. From the early 1560s, and particularly after Parker's 'Advertisements' of 1566, the term can be used, however loosely, to refer to those opponents of the Elizabethan Settlement of 1559 [3.2–3.4].

If one thing can be said to have linked Puritans together it was a view of the Church stripped of external ornamentation. Whereas both Catholics and to a lesser extent Anglicans laid emphasis on the visual elements in church services, Puritans believed in the supremacy of the spoken word and laid emphasis on lectures and sermons. Some Puritans could not accept the hierarchical structure and believed in the Presbyterian system. They were never numerous, even if propaganda gave them a louder voice than their numbers warranted. Separatists believed in the importance of each individual congregation and rejected the notion of a national Church, but they were also few in number.

Puritanism required a greater intellectual effort on the part of the listener and thus had less impact among the poor and illiterate. This aspect was accentuated by the support Puritans enjoyed from powerful Court patrons like Huntingdon, Bedford and, most of all, Leicester. It is a common misconception to equate Puritanism with capitalism, as M. M. Knappen shows, by emphasising Puritanism as an 'other-worldly' belief, suspicious of capitalist tendencies. The fact that Puritans were to be found in the merchant classes was more a reflection of their social origins than their economic activities.

The views of Thomas Cartwright on Presbyterianism presented a challenge to Royal Supremacy in the Church [3.9]. He declared that the idea of bishops appointed by the civil power had no basis in Scripture. Although Cartwright was forced to give up his professorship at Cambridge, the battle was taken up in the House of Commons which contained a growing number of Puritan members. In 1571 William Strickland introduced a bill to reform the Prayer Book and bring it back to the teachings of the early Church. Elizabeth at once banned the Commons from discussing religious bills before they had been considered by the clergy.

During the 1580s, Puritans and Presbyterians organised classes or synods: conferences of local clergy based on the Swiss and German models. In the forefront of this movement was John Field, a London cleric and part-author of the *Admonition to Parliament* of 1572. Failing to make any progress towards reform by parliamentary measures, the Puritans resorted to printing pamphlets, but Elizabeth retaliated by issuing a Star Chamber decree for the control of printing presses. Archbishop Whitgift undertook a drive towards conformity in the Church, using the Court of High Commission to destroy the strength of Presbyterian organisation in the 1590s [3.14 and 3.15]. Nevertheless, more general Puritan attitudes were widely spread across society by 1603.

Elizabeth and the Catholic threat

It was assumed in 1558 that Elizabeth would marry and that her consort would have an important say in the religion of England thereafter. As a result, her Protestant advisers feared that the religious changes of 1559 would not prove permanent.

Although the large majority of the clergy took the Oath of Supremacy to Elizabeth, the bishops were soon reporting to the Privy Council that Catholic ceremonials were strong at grass roots level [4.1 and 4.2]. They were encountering resistance from amongst the gentry, many of whom had maintained their previous positions of rank in local communities as Sheriffs and Justices. It proved difficult to ensure the removal of rood lofts and Catholic ornaments, which were concealed, and restored as soon as the opportunity arose. As required by the Act of Uniformity, most Catholics attended church rather than pay the fine, though some gentry refused and were accounted 'recusants'. However, Elizabeth was apparently satisfied by outward conformity and obedience and Catholics were not much persecuted during the first decade of her rule.

The Pope gave little leadership to English Catholics during the 1560s, probably because Philip II preferred to see Elizabeth rule in England, rather than Mary Stuart, who would have extended the power of France across the English Channel. However, the flight of Mary Stuart to England in 1568, and the sudden breakdown in relations between England and Spain in the same year, brought on a crisis which seriously affected the condition of English Catholics.

The outbreak of the Northern Revolt in 1569, using religion as a pretext to win the support of the people, was the first in a series of attempts to overthrow Elizabeth and replace her with Mary Stuart [4.5]. After the Papal Bull of 1570 Catholics were faced with a clash of loyalties between their religion and their ruler [4.6]. This difficult choice was expressed by Burghley when he equated loyalty to the Pope with treason against Elizabeth, and during the 1570s the government began to impose stricter controls on Catholic recusants.

Though Catholicism had remained strong in some parts of the South, notably Sussex, its strength rested in remote areas of the North and West, where feudal ties to local magnates were strong. Professor Bossy argues that after 1558 Catholicism survived in three ways. In the wild border areas of Scotland and Wales local magnates could still attract strong personal allegiance. In other inaccessible areas, particularly in the North, there were small but independent seigneurial households, within which the ceremonies of the Catholic Church were conducted without hindrance. Throughout the rest of the country there were numerous large, though scattered, households to which recusant priests could come for help and even, on occasions, for employment as domestic chaplains [4.4]. Indeed, in 1581 Lord Vaux declared that his house was a parish in itself, to which all his servants and tenants could come to hear mass. This may seem a very dangerous declaration for a Catholic to make, yet Elizabeth had little to fear from the Catholic gentry, who played no significant part in the 1569 revolt or the various plots against her.

A far greater threat came from missionary priests, who came to England after 1574 from the seminary founded at Douai in the Netherlands by Father William Allen. These young Catholics, inspired by the teachings of the Counter-Reformation, were willing to give their lives in the struggle to win back the country to true religion [4.10]. In 1580 they were joined by Jesuits like Robert Parsons and Edmund Campion. Their arrival coincided with a deteriorating situation abroad, following the assassination of William the Silent in 1584 and the decision by Elizabeth to send troops to the Netherlands. Thus, although they protested that their purpose was spiritual and not political, these missionary priests could not avoid being in the front line of a war.

Elizabeth's government passed stricter recusancy laws in 1581, increasing fines for non-attendance from twelve pence to twenty pounds. It also increased its action against Catholic priests, and more than a hundred were condemned to death for treason [4.12]. They died as martyrs for their faith and yet by the standards of the time their crime was political and not religious. They threatened the Royal Supremacy and, backed by Spain and the Pope, they also threatened the safety of the realm. In his polemical writings William Allen encouraged Catholics to overthrow their ruler, but there was never any likelihood that the majority of English Catholics would be anything but loyal to Elizabeth, in spite of some government fears.

Historian C. Haigh has recently pointed to weaknesses in the missionary effort. After leaving their seminaries at Douai, Rheims and Rome, most of the priests entered England through southern ports like Dover and Rye and this made them concentrate in areas where there were fewer Catholics. By 1580 half of all missionaries were in Essex, London and the Thames Valley, where fewer than twenty per cent of Catholics lived, whereas areas ripe for a Catholic revival, like Cumbria and Wales, were allowed to slump into conformity. Moreover, Allen's aim was to concentrate his efforts on the gentry, who would provide the leadership of any restoration of Catholicism, as well as persuade their servants and tenants to follow the faith. The Jesuits saw restoration in terms of a seigneurial rather than a congregational revival and inadequate attention was paid to the lower orders, many of whom were desperate for Catholic preaching and confession.

Nevertheless, though Catholicism made converts, even during the difficult years of the 1580s, it no longer posed a threat to the security of the new Church or the supremacy of the monarch. By 1603 it was estimated that there were some 8,570 recusants, as well as 100,000 who attended church occasionally in order to avoid fines.

Elizabeth and the local communities

The extension of the powers of central government over the local communities and the opposition encountered there is a main theme in Elizabethan history. Regionalism and localism were very strong throughout England, particularly in counties like Devon and Cornwall. The majority of people referred to their home county as their 'cuntrie', and for the labouring classes this was the extent of their world. Within local communities the landowning gentry formed a natural ruling class, and it was these people who, as Justices or Sheriffs, conducted much of the government of their localities [5.6]. During Elizabeth's reign their functions increased greatly and these people were recruited to assist with numerous commissions into such diverse subjects as recusancy, subsidies, the Poor Law and drainage.

The office of Sheriff, so important in the Middle Ages, had declined in Tudor times. Some of its tasks had been taken over by the Justices of the Peace, but the really important Tudor innovation had been the creation of the Lord Lieutenancy. The absence of a standing army and the recurrent threat of internal revolt or foreign invasion meant that central government had to be able to organise the mustering of county forces. The Trained Bands were created in 1573 in reaction to the Northern Revolt of 1569 but by the 1580s there was a need to organise forces for service abroad [5.2]. By 1585 every county had a Lord Lieutenant, whose role was essentially military, concerned with the levying, training and equipping of the militia [5.1].

It was common for local communities to resent the costs involved, and to supply the poorest, weakest soldiers they could find, often selecting vagrant or criminals [5.3 and 5.4]. In view of the poor standard of recruits, it is hardly surprising that there was a constant threat of public disorder, and from 1588 the Provost Marshall was empowered to use martial law on disorderly soldiers.

During Elizabeth's reign the numbers of Justices of the Peace increased significantly: a reflection of the status associated with the office by local gentry. Nevertheless, the task was no easy one. Justices had to cope with a great quantity of complex legislation, individually on occasions, or together in Quarter Sessions, when all the Justices of the shire were supposed to assemble. It was on these occasions that important local matters were resolved, including the fixing of wage rates and the supervision of Poor Law legislation.

The Justices were unpaid servants of the crown and it was not unknown for some of them to act corruptly. The Privy Council exercised a supervisory role over their work and there are many examples of conflict between central and local authority. On the subject of 'Ship Money' there were occasions when both Justices and the Deputy Lieutenants proved obstructionist and against such united opposition, it was often impossible for the Queen to prevail [5.5]. Furthermore the collection of the parliamentary subsidy was riddled with corruption, which she could only condemn but not reform. Her rule was based on consent and her capacity to enforce decisions was limited.

The Elizabethan Poor Law represented a notable achievement and the codification of 1601 was to last over two centuries. The 'poor rate' was a compulsory assessment in each parish, which financed outdoor relief to deserving households. However, there was always a shortage of money and from 1563 the Justices were empowered to imprison those who refused to contribute when requested. From 1573 it was the task of the Justices to assess contributions. Efforts were also made to reduce the number of vagrants and beggars by providing work for them or, after

1598, by whipping them back to their own parish [5.12]. In genuine cases Justices could provide materials for work and erect a house of correction.

In the second half of Elizabeth's reign, people in authority felt threatened by the increasing number of paupers and vagrants and their effect on society [5.8]. In an attempt to combat this there were numerous bills in Parliament aimed at improving the condition and the behaviour of the poor [5.14]. Probably most of the vagrants were genuinely unemployed and merely seeking jobs, but it was difficult for contemporaries to understand the economic forces which were causing the suffering. In some ways the Tudor Poor Law is more impressive on paper than it was in practice. Justices often failed in their duties to levy the poor rate and usually only did so in times of emergency. Often it was left to private charity to sustain the poor of the parish. Nevertheless, though the legislation of the Elizabethan period had obvious weaknesses, it was a first step towards creating a system of local responsibility for community problems.

Elizabeth's financial problems

It is greatly to Elizabeth's credit that, with the assistance of Sir Thomas Gresham, she was able to pay off her inherited debts to the Antwerp exchange and to begin a revaluation of the currency after the disastrous debasement under Henry VIII and Edward VI [6.1]. In these ways Elizabeth established a reputation abroad as a sound financial risk, while giving her government a feeling of greater strength and permanence [6.2 and 6.3]. In France and Spain, monarchs showed that expensive foreign wars would lead a country to bankruptcy. After her early involvement in Scotland and France, Elizabeth avoided war until in 1585 it could be avoided no more. She took the measures recommended by the best economists available and, if these were not effective, it was more due to the inflation from which all European states of the time suffered.

However, conservatism, so effective in some areas of government, was unsuited to the crucial area of finance. The Elizabethan administrative machine suffered from the conservative outlook of its two most prominent members: Elizabeth herself and Burghley. The Queen was suspicious of innovation and Burghley, as Lord Treasurer after 1572, missed the opportunity of carrying out financial reforms which could have provided the Queen with money to finance foreign involvement and reduce her dependence on parliamentary finance. The increasing costs required an active rather than a passive approach and the tendency to cut back, to conserve and to play the miser on occasions, did little to improve returns from the various sources of royal revenue.

Burghley failed to exploit the Crown's ordinary revenue, like rents from royal lands, feudal revenues, first fruits and profits from justice, and only occasionally kept charges in line with inflation. Furthermore, returns from customs dues were disappointing. Methods of assessment were frequently outdated: some dues like cloth and imported wines were assessed on quantity rather than value, while others used a scale of values unchanged since Mary's reign. The outcome was a shortfall for the Crown which had to be made up in some other way. The revenues from Crown lands suffered a similar under-assessment, especially considering the fast rise in food prices. It is noticeable that, when Sir Robert Cecil succeeded his father as Master of the Wards, he achieved a substantial rise in the revenue from wardships.

Elizabeth usually called on Parliament when she needed money but parliamentary subsidies produced disappointing returns, partly because they were unequal in their incidence and partly because their collection was subject to corruption and maladministration [6.5–6.7]. Elizabeth shared with Burghley the desire to keep taxes low, in order to maintain the support of merchants and rich tenants. However, such under-taxation had both long and short term effects. In the long term it meant that English tax-payers became accustomed to paying only a small part of their income in taxation and resented any request to pay more. In the short term, of course, it meant that the Crown was always in need of cash and had to exploit extra-parliamentary forms of taxation, like 'Ship Money' and Privy Seal loans. Under Elizabeth these practices were grudgingly accepted, but under her successors they were to be a source of endless trouble.

Consequently, although Elizabeth and Burghley maintained the Crown's solvency in the face of enormous financial demands from the wars in Ireland, the Low Countries, and at sea, they lacked the vision to modernise an outdated financial machine.

Between 1510 and 1620 prices rose rapidly in Europe but the study of economics had not yet reached a stage when price inflation could be understood. Many contemporary explanations were offered. Some assumed it was the result of simple greed on the part of profiteering middlemen, avaricious landlords or overpaid labourers. During Elizabeth's reign a purely English solution was sought in the currency revaluation of 1561. It was assumed that prices would fall immediately but, when they failed to do so, it was realised that debasement was not the cause of inflation but merely a means of fuelling it. By the 1570s thinkers like Sir Thomas Smith had concluded that the inflow into Europe of bullion from the Spanish possessions in the New World was increasing prices [**6.10 and 6.12**]. However, this could not explain why the prices increasing most rapidly were those of home-grown foods and grain.

Among modern historians, the most widely held explanation is that the rapid growth of population put pressure on subsistence foods like cheap grains, by increasing demand for a commodity in limited supply. This pressure was further increased during the 1590s, as a result of a series of poor harvests. As money decreased in value, Crown revenue fell disastrously, as much of it depended on fixed income. The poor suffered particularly during the bad harvests and dearth of the 1590s, adding to the general dissatisfaction at the end of Elizabeth's reign [**6.13**].

Elizabeth's Legacy

The period between the Armada and the end of Elizabeth's reign saw a breakdown in the system of administration which, with the assistance of her Councillors, particularly William Cecil, the Queen had struggled so hard to establish. Elizabeth was losing popularity because of the harsh social and economic conditions of the 1590s, and the indecisive and expensive war with Spain. The decline of the patronage system heralded a new generation of corrupt public servants. Opposition in Parliament to government policy had barely been kept in check despite the skilful control of debates by her Privy Councillors, and by the awe in which she herself was held.

There would be no such concessions to her successors. The need for war finances revealed the inadequacy of the Elizabethan governmental system and created tensions in the local communities, which were a warning to future monarchs that foreign wars should be avoided. Inflationary pressures exacerbated the natural disasters of the 1590s to impose an even greater burden of unemployment and starvation on the working masses. In religious affairs, the threat from extreme Protestantism had been overcome by 1603. But there were new dangers of ideological splits within the Church of England, with the concept of the *de jure* episcopacy, that bishops were essential to the true Church, and the attack on Calvinist predestination. In foreign affairs James inherited an unpopular war with Spain and an Ireland, sullen, resentful, but firmly under English control. If England was not an ungovernable realm it was a realm which needed the most delicate handling.

A note on sources

In the following selection of documents, twentieth-century spelling and punctuation are used, and foreign documents have been translated into English. The vocabulary has not been modernised, but there are footnotes to explain words or phrases whose meaning is ambiguous or unclear.

Below are two versions of the same document, from 'Acts of the Privy Council', 1589, which show the way in which primary sources may be treated:

(i)   Photograph of an extract of the original document, now kept in the
      Public Record Office, London

(ii)

xxjth of July 1589. Lres sent unto the commissioners appointed for
the Assessement of the Subsedies within the severall counties of
Somersett [and 32 others] . . . wch were deliv'ed to be dispersed
accordingly by John Unett one of the messingers of her Ma'tie's
Chamber . . . yet considering the notable & evident abasing, and
diminucion of manie men's values heretofore in their Assessem'tes
under all reasonable proporcions, sp'ially of men of the better stat of
livelehood and countenaunce, and therewth also in manie shires and
devisions suche negligence or in some p'tes apparance of corrupcion
for privat gaine, that was used in choyce of the headcollectours, as in
many places of the Realme the collectors dyd not aunswer their
collecons at the tymes appointed by the space of manie yeares, untill
they were thereto forced by sondry processes, and some have not as
yett aunswered anie p'te thereof, and some others have in their
excuse, being comitted to prison, alledged that their mrs by whome
they were named had p'te of their colleccon in their owne hands, and
some others have ben named of soe meane livinges, contrary to the
Statute, as their hath ben noe meanes to recov' of them their debts.

A strict transcription of the document, keeping to the original spelling and
punctuation

A modernised version of this document can be found on p. 108–9 **[6.5]**.
Consider the advantages and disadvantages of this procedure of
modernisation.

1 The Settlement of 1559

Elizabeth came to the throne after thirty years of religious upheaval which had threatened the unity of the realm, leaving it weak and divided. She was no innovator in either politics or religion, yet change was necessary, and she faced dangers from both entrenched Catholics and Protestant zealots. To restore unity and strength she realised that she had to achieve a religious settlement which would gain the assent, if not necessarily the approval, of most believers in the country.

Elizabeth's accession had been a signal for the return to England of many Protestant exiles, who had fled her sister Mary's persecution and had found refuge in Strasbourg, Zurich, Frankfurt and Geneva. The threat posed by these returning exiles alarmed even moderate Catholics, like Archbishop Heath, who saw the country 'overwhelmed and drowned in the waters of schism, sects and divisions'. In his funeral oration for Queen Mary, Bishop White made reference to the returning exiles: 'The wolves be coming out of Geneva and have sent their books before, full of pestilent doctrines'.

Along with the returning English Protestants came continental reformers too, who were determined to inflame passions for the religious changes they expected in England. These English and continental Protestants crowded into London and began 'to sow abroad the doctrine of the gospel more freely, first in private houses and then in churches, and the people greedy of novelties began to flock unto them in great number and to wrangle amongst themselves and with the papists, about questions controverted in religion'.

In the early months of her reign Elizabeth tried to control the excesses of these Protestant extremists, for fear of losing the support of moderate opinion for her religious changes. The Venetian, Il Schifanoya, describes the religious climate in England at the time of Elizabeth's accession in his letter to Vivaldino, the Mantuan ambassador to King Philip II of Spain:

1.1

> Until now I had believed that the matters of religion would continue
> in the accustomed manner, her Majesty having promised this with
> her own mouth many times; but now I have lost faith, and I see that
> little by little they are returning to the bad use. On Christmas day

the Bishop of Carlisle sang high mass, and her Majesty sent to tell 5
him that he was not to elevate the host; to which the good Bishop
replied that thus he had learnt the mass, and that she must pardon
him as he could not do otherwise; so the Gospel being ended, her
Majesty rose and departed, and on other days it has been so done by
her chaplains. 10

    On the same day in the church of St Augustine . . . two
individuals (whom I will not call preachers, for they were mechanics
and cobblers), followed by a very great mob, entered by force,
breaking the locks of the doors. both of them leaped into the pulpit,
and, book in hand, commenced reading and preaching to the people, 15
one following the other, uttering a thousand ribaldries concerning the
reign of the blessed memory of Queen Mary and of the Cardinal.

**Il Schifanoya to Vivaldino, 31 December 1558, in *Calendar of State
Papers Venetian*, 1558, p. 2**

It was to combat this sort of behaviour on the part of the Protestants and
their supporters, and to maintain public order, that Elizabeth had the
following proclamation read:

1.2

The Queen's Majesty . . . has . . . thought it necessary to charge and
command . . . all manner of her subjects, as well those that be called
to ministry in the Church as all others, that they do forbear to preach
or teach, or to give audience to[1] any manner of doctrine or preaching,
other than to the gospels and epistles commonly called the gospel and 5
epistle of the day, and to the Ten Commandments in the vulgar
tongue[2] without exposition or addition of any manner, sense or
meaning to be applied or added; or to use any other manner of public
prayer, rite or ceremony in the Church but that which is already used
at this present in her Majesty's own chapel, and the Lord's Prayer 10
and the Creed in English, until consultation may be held by
Parliament, by her Majesty and her three estates of this realm, for the
better conciliation and accord of such causes as at this present are
moved in matters and ceremonies of religion.

[1] 'to give audience to' = to listen to
[2] 'the vulgar tongue' = everyday language

**Royal Proclamation, 27 December 1558, also in P. L. Hughes and
J. F. Larkin (eds.), *Tudor Royal Proclamations*, vol. 2, pp. 102–3**

The Queen made it clear that she intended to proceed with the support of Parliament in matters of religion, and yet speed was essential if serious unrest was to be avoided. It seemed likely that most of the House of Commons would be willing to follow Elizabeth into Protestantism. However, in the House of Lords the bishops would strongly oppose any settlement on Protestant lines.

Parliament was opened on 25 January 1559, in an atmosphere of uncertainty tinged with expectation. Il Schifanoya was an observer that day, as the Queen made her progress first to Westminster Abbey:

1.3

On arriving at Westminster Abbey, the Abbot, robed pontifically, with all his monks in procession, each of them having a lighted torch in his hand, received her as usual, giving her first of all incense and holy water; and when her Majesty saw the monks with the torches, she said, 'Away with those torches, for we see very well'; and her   5
choristers singing the litany in English, she was accompanied to the high altar under her canopy.

Thereupon Dr Cox, a married priest, who has hitherto been beyond the sea, ascended the pulpit and preached the sermon, in which, after saying many things freely against the monks, proving by   10
his arguments that they ought to be persecuted and punished by her Majesty, as they were impious for having caused the burning of so many poor innocents under pretext of heresy, on which he expatiated greatly; he then commenced praising her Majesty, saying amongst other things that God had given her this dignity to the end that she   15
might no longer allow or tolerate the past iniquities; exhorting her to destroy the images of the saints, the churches, the monasteries, and all other things dedicated to divine worship . . . The sermon lasted an hour and a half, the peers standing the whole time, after which they went to the place prepared for the Parliament.

Il Schifanoya to Vivaldino, 30 January 1559, in *Calendar of State Papers Venetian*, 1559, pp. 22–3

There were those in London who were willing to take Dr Cox at his word, as Il Schifanoya later informed the Castellan of Mantua:

1.4

> . . . the farce performed in the presence of her Majesty on the day of
> the Epiphany, and I not having sufficient intellect to interpret it, nor
> yet the mummery performed after supper on the same day, of crows
> in the habits of Cardinals, of asses habited as Bishops, and of wolves
> representing Abbots. I will consign it to silence, as also the new   5
> commencement of ritual made in her Majesty's Chapel with the
> English litanies, which omit St Mary, all the Saints, the Pope and the
> Dead. Nor will I record the levities and unusual licentiousness
> practised at Court in dances and banquets, nor the masquerade of
> friars in the streets of London . . .

Il Schifanoya to the Castellan of Mantua, 23 January 1559, in
Calendar of State Papers Venetian, **1559, p. 11**

Questions

1   Explain the meaning and/or significance of the following:
   (i) 'he was not to elevate the host' [1.1, **line 6**]
  (ii) 'her three estates of this realm' [1.2, **line 12**]
 (iii) 'robed pontifically' [1.3, **line 1**]
 (iv) 'a married priest' [1.3, **line 8**]?
2   What do we learn from documents **1.1** to **1.4** about Elizabeth's
religious preferences?
3   How reliable do you think Il Schifanoya's reports are [**1.1, 1.3 and
1.4**]?
4   Is there any evidence in documents **1.1** to **1.4** of the influence of
continental Protestantism on the Settlement of 1559?
5   Comment on the significance of Elizabeth's decision to settle religion
after consultation 'by Parliament, by her Majesty and her three
estates of this realm' [1.2, **line 12**].
6   Do documents **1.1** to **1.4** suggest that a 'Protestant' settlement was 'a
foregone conclusion'?

Elizabeth's religious Settlement was of concern to more than just her own
subjects. On the continent, rulers both temporal and secular anxiously
awaited news of the Settlement. Here was an event of European
significance, particularly to England's ally, Philip II of Spain. Even while
Parliament was debating a new Act of Supremacy, negotiations had re-
started with France, at Cateau Cambresis, to end the disastrous war which,
under Mary, had cost England the port of Calais. The threat of the Franco-

Scottish union was very real to Elizabeth in 1559, and the need to maintain friendship with Spain undoubtedly contributed to the air of caution which marked the beginning of her reign. Philip of Spain still thought that marriage to Elizabeth would be the likeliest way of cementing relations between the two countries, but news of religious unrest in England disturbed him. In 1559 he wrote to Count de Feria, his ambassador in London:

1.5

> I have decided that as soon as you receive this you will seek the best
> opportunity you can to see the Queen and tell her from me that as a
> good and true brother who really wishes her well both on account of
> our relationship and because I desire to see her firmly and peacefully
> established on the throne, I must warn her to ponder and consider   5
> deeply the evils which may result in England from a change in
> religion, particularly thus early in her reign, and the dissensions and
> perturbations which may arise therefrom; and I therefore beg and
> entreat her to hold her hand and not to allow any innovations seeing
> how much the preservation and stability of the state depend on it . . . 10
> but if notwithstanding all your efforts you can see that they still go
> on with their intention, and that you can obtain no success in that
> way, you had better consider whether it will not be well to press the
> Queen by saying that if this change is made all idea of my marriage
> with her must be broken off, and if she has any thoughts of this   15
> marriage this may be efficacious.
>
> **Philip II to Count de Feria, 12 February 1559, in** *Calendar of State*
> *Papers Spanish*, **1559, pp. 26–9**

Count de Feria worked assiduously for his master, earning the hatred of Elizabeth's Protestant advisers. However, he under-estimated the Queen's diplomatic skill. It seems unlikely that she ever intended to marry King Philip, but she was not willing to dismiss his suit while England was in such a weak situation abroad. Count de Feria reported developments to Philip:

1.6

> The Queen . . . said after a time that she could not marry your
> Majesty as she was a heretic. I was much surprised to hear her use
> such words and begged her to tell me the cause of so great a change

since last I discussed the subject with her, but she did not enlighten
me.   5
    These heretics, and the devil that prompts them are so careful to
leave no stone unturned to compass their ends that no doubt they
have persuaded her that your Majesty wishes to marry her for
religious objects alone, and so she kept repeating to me that she was
heretical and consequently could not marry your Majesty. She was so   10
disturbed and excited and so resolved to restore religion as her father
left it, that at last I said that I did not consider her heretical and
could not believe that she would sanction the things which were
being discussed in Parliament, because if she changed the religion she
would be ruined, and that your Majesty would not separate from the   15
union of the church for all the kingdoms of the earth. She said then
much less would he do it for a woman. I did not want to be all
rigour, so I said that men did more for a woman than for anything
else. She said she would not take the title of head of the Church, but
that so much money was taken out of the country for the Pope every   20
year that she must put an end to it, and that the Bishops were lazy
poltroons. I replied that the poltroons were the preachers she listened
to, and that it added little to her honour and was a great scandal that
so many rogues should come from Germany, and get into the pulpit
before her and great congregations to preach a thousand absurdities   25
without being learned or worthy to be listened to. After we had been
talking for half an hour Knollys came in and said supper was ready, a
new thing, and as I think arranged by those who are working this
wickedness for there is nothing that annoys them more than that I
should speak to her. I took my leave saying that she was not the   30
Elizabeth that I knew.

**Count de Feria to Philip II, 19 March 1559, in *Calendar of State
Papers Spanish*, 1559, pp. 37–8**

Questions

1   Comment on the significance of Feria's report that Elizabeth
     'resolved to restore religion as her father left it.' [1.6, line 11]
2   What do 1.5 and 1.6 tell us about Spanish policy at this time?
3   What do you suppose de Feria meant by 'she was not the Elizabeth
     that I knew' [1.6, lines 30–1]?
4   Do documents 1.5 and 1.6 modify any of the conclusions you had
     reached after examining documents 1.1 to 1.4?

Elizabeth's attempt to win the support of some of the Marian bishops received a setback when Convocation, under Bonner's leadership, confirmed its support for Papal Supremacy and the doctrine of transubstantiation. Clearly she could expect no help from this quarter. In fact, she and her Council had badly miscalculated the strength of opposition in the Upper House and, with Easter approaching, there seemed little likelihood that the necessary changes in religion could be passed before the recess.

As the supreme law-making body in the realm, Parliament had been involved in much time-consuming legislation, trying to sort out the muddle over Church lands and property. Elizabeth decided therefore to continue Parliament after Holy Week, in an attempt to achieve the Royal Supremacy and a Protestant settlement.

The Act of Supremacy was now passed, and Elizabeth was recognised as Supreme Governor of the Church. Royal officials and clergy were required to take an oath of obedience to Elizabeth, Mary's heresy laws were repealed and the celebration of Communion in both kinds was confirmed.

1.7

> IX   And for the better observation and maintenance of this Act, may it please your Highness that it may be further enacted by the authority aforesaid[1] that all and every archbishop, bishop and all and every other ecclesiastical person . . . shall make, take and receive a corporal oath upon the evangelist[2], before such person or persons as   5
> shall please your Highness . . . I, A.B., do utterly testify and declare in my conscience, that the Queen's Highness is the only Supreme Governor of this realm . . . as well in all spiritual or ecclesiastical things or causes as temporal, and that no foreign prince, person, prelate, state or potentate has or ought to have any jurisdiction,   10
> power, superiority, pre-eminence or authority ecclesiastical or spiritual within this realm . . . and do promise that from henceforth I shall bear faith and true allegiance to the Queen's Highness.
>
> [1] 'the authority aforesaid' = that of Queen and Parliament
> [2] 'a corporal oath upon the evangelist' = an oath sworn while holding one of the four gospels

Act of Supremacy, 1559, in *Statutes of the Realm*, vol. 4 (i), p. 352

The Catholic reaction in the House of Lords was predictably hostile. Archbishop Heath, ironically mirroring the attitude of John Knox in *The First Blast of the Trumpet against the Monstrous Regiment of Women*, a tract which had enraged Elizabeth, spoke out strongly against the Act of Supremacy:

1.8

> A woman, in the degree [= hierarchy] of Christ's church, is not
> called to be an apostle, nor evangelist, nor to be a shepherd, neither a
> doctor or preacher. Therefore she cannot be supreme head of Christ's
> militant [= evangelical] church, nor yet of any part thereof.
>
> **Archbishop Heath, 18 March 1559, in J. Strype, *Annals*, vol. 1 (ii),
> pp. 399–407**

Bishop Scot of Chester questioned Parliament's authority to act in a purely
religious issue:

1.9

> And if our religion, as it was here of late discreetly [= moderately],
> godly and learnedly declared, does consist partly in inward things, in
> faith, hope, charity, and partly in outward things, as in common
> prayer and the holy sacraments universally administered. Now, as
> concerning these outward things, this bill does clearly in very deed   5
> extinguish them, setting in their places I know not what. And the
> inward it does also shake, that it leaves them very bare and feeble.
> And as for the certainty of our faith, whereof the story of the church
> does speak, a thing of all others most necessary, if it shall hang upon
> an Act of Parliament we have but a weak staff to lean unto. And that   10
> I shall desire you to take me here not as to speak in derogation of the
> authority of Parliament, which I knowledge [= acknowledge] to be of
> great strength in matters whereto it extends. But for matters of
> religion, I do not think it ought to meddle withal.
>
> **Bishop Scot of Chester against the Supremacy Bill, 1559, also in C.
> Cross, *The Royal Supremacy in the Elizabethan Church*, p. 122**

Elizabeth had needed complete co-operation in the House of Commons to
achieve the passage of the Act of Supremacy. Even so, Conservatives in the
House of Lords managed to protect themselves by stipulating that nothing
could be judged heresy, unless declared so by the authority of Scripture or
the first four general councils. Some of the frustration felt by the Protestant
reformers can be seen in the following extract, a letter from Bishop Jewel to
the reformer Peter Martyr:

1.10

It has happened that the mass in many places has of itself fallen to
the ground, without any laws for its discontinuance. If the queen
herself would but banish it from her private chapel, the whole thing
might be easily got rid of . . . She has, however, so regulated this
mass of hers (which she has hitherto retained only for the   5
circumstances of the times) that although many things are done
therein, which are scarcely to be endured, it may yet be heard
without any great danger. But this woman, excellent as she is, and
earnest in the cause of true religion, notwithstanding she desires a
thorough change as early as possible, cannot however be induced to   10
effect such change without the effect of law . . . Meanwhile, many
alterations in religion are effected in parliament, in spite of the
opposition and gainsaying of the bishops.

Jewel to Martyr, 14 April 1559, in *Zurich Letters I*, vol. 1, p. 18

Questions

1   Why do you suppose that Elizabeth abandoned the claim of her
    father and brother to be Supreme Head of the Church, and became
    instead 'Supreme Governor' [1.7, lines 7–8]?
2   Does document 1.8 confirm or contradict the impressions you have
    gained from other documents in this chapter about the disadvantages
    Elizabeth suffered from being a female head of state?
3   Why do you suppose that Bishop Scot felt that Parliament ought not
    to meddle in matters of religion [1.9]?
4   Explain and comment on Jewel's remark that Elizabeth 'cannot
    however be induced to effect such change without the effect of law'
    [1.10, lines 10–11]?

The Act of Uniformity (1559) came very close to defeat in the House of
Lords. The bishops were united in their opposition and many lay peers,
although willing to break with Rome, were unhappy to accept the 1552
Prayer Book, which rejected transubstantiation. A compromise was
eventually reached by which the 1552 Prayer Book was reimposed, but
with significant amendments in a conservative direction. Most crucially, a
deliberate ambiguity was introduced at the heart of the Communion. In
1549 the words that the priest said when giving bread (i) and administer-
ing the cup of wine (ii) were:

1.11(a)

> (i) The body of Our Lord Jesus Christ which was given for thee, preserve thy body and soul unto everlasting life.
>
> (ii) The blood of Our Lord Jesus Christ which was shed for thee, preserve thy body and soul unto everlasting life.

The Book of Common Prayer, 1549

This formula was intended to imply the Real Presence of Christ in the bread and wine. In 1552 the formulae were changed:

1.11(b)

> (i) Take and eat this in remembrance that Christ died for thee and be thankful.
>
> (ii) Drink this in remembrance that Christ's blood was shed for thee and be thankful.

The Book of Common Prayer, 1552

This was intended to suggest that the Communion was a memorial of Christ's Passion, and to deny the Real Presence. In the 1559 Prayer Book the priest was to run together the 1549 and 1552 formulae, leaving everyone to conclude what they wished.

Thus the Act of Uniformity was built around a compromise:

1.12

> And . . . be it enacted by the Queen's Highness . . . that all and
> singular ministers in any cathedral or parish church . . . be bound to
> say and use the matins, evensong, celebration of the Lord's Supper¹,
> and administration of each of the sacraments and all their common
> and open [= public] prayer in such order and form as is mentioned   5
> in the said Book so authorised by Parliament in the said fifth and
> sixth year of the reign of King Edward the Sixth, with one alteration
> or addition of certain lessons to be used on every Sunday in the year,
> and the form of the litany altered and corrected, and two sentences
> only added in the delivery of the sacrament to the communicants and   10
> none other or otherwise . . . From and after the said feast . . . all and

every person and persons inhabiting within this realm . . . shall
diligently and faithfully . . . resort to their parish church or chapel
accustomed . . . upon every Sunday and other days ordained and
used to be kept as holy days, and then and there to abide orderly and 15
soberly during the time of the Common Prayer, preachings or other
service of God . . . upon pain of punishment by the censures of the
Church, and also upon pain that every person so offending shall
forfeit for every such offence twelve pence, to be levied by the
churchwardens . . . to the use of the poor of the same parish.   20

[1] 'The Lord's Supper' = Holy Communion

Act of Uniformity, 1559, in *Statutes of the Realm*, vol. 4, pp. 355–8

Additionally, Clause XII of the Act stated that:

1.13

. . . such ornaments of the church and of the ministers shall be
retained and be in use as was in the Church of England, by authority
of Parliament, in the second year of the reign of King Edward the
Sixth, until other order shall be therein taken [= given] by the
authority of the Queen's Majesty.

Act of Uniformity, 1559, in *Statutes of the Realm*, vol. 4, p. 355–8

The restoration of clerical vestments was a blow to the Protestant
reformers but one which at first they did not regard as permanent. Later
the matter was to grow into a great controversy. Edmund Sandys,
apparently misjudging the strength of the Queen's own convictions,
summed up the views of the reformers to Matthew Parker, soon to become
Elizabeth's Archbishop of Canterbury:

1.14

The last book of service is gone through with a proviso to retain the
ornaments which were used in the first and second years of King
Edward, until it pleases the queen to take other order for them. Our
gloss upon this text is that we shall not be forced to use them, but
that others in the meantime shall not convey them away but that they 5
may remain for the queen . . .
Nothing has been enacted about the marriage of the clergy but so far

left in the air. Lever was married now of late. The queen's majesty will wink at it but not establish it by law, which is nothing but to bastard our children.

Sandys to Parker, 30 April 1559, in J. Bruce and T. Perowne (eds.)
Correspondence of Matthew Parker, **1853, pp. 65–6**

Questions

1   What is the significance of the fusion of formulae from the 1549 and 1552 Prayer Books as given in documents **1.11a** and **1.11b**?
2   Do documents **1.11** to **1.14** suggest that the whole Settlement was a compromise which left the Church 'but half reformed'?
3   Describe and comment on the tone of Sandys' letter to Parker [**1.14**].
4   Is the 1559 Settlement the kind of settlement that earlier documents in this chapter had led you to expect?

Within a month of the end of Parliament, Elizabeth and her advisers were ready to begin the implementation of the Settlement. The Oath of Supremacy was to be imposed by the newly-established Court of High Commission. All but one of the Marian bishops refused to take the oath, and they were deprived of office. On the other hand, a very small number of the lower clergy – perhaps as low as four per cent – refused to take the Oath.

The Commissioners also enforced a set of royal injunctions, which clearly owed much to Elizabeth's determination to establish a sound basis for the national Church. The clergy were ordered to wear 'such seemly habits, garments and such square caps' as were used in King Edward's day, while clerical marriage, though permitted, was discouraged. In the Injunctions of 1559 Elizabeth stipulated that:

1.15

. . . no manner of priest or deacon shall hereafter take to his wife any manner of woman without the advice or allowance first had upon good examination by the bishop of the same diocese, and two justices of the peace of the same shire . . .

Royal Injunctions, 1559, in A. Sparrow, *A Collection of Articles,*
Injunctions, Canons . . . of the Church of England, **1661, pp. 63–80**

Elizabeth would have preferred a celibate clergy. In choosing Matthew Parker as Archbishop of Canterbury she knew that she was compromising her views, but most of the Marian exiles were married and to have resisted clerical marriage altogether in 1559 would have cost her the services of many able men. However, with her own very personal views on marriage, Elizabeth was unable to subdue her true feelings for very long. During her Progress in Suffolk and Essex in 1561 she was so angered by what she saw that she issued the following Injunction:

1.16

The Queen's Majesty, considering how the palaces and houses of Cathedral Churches and Colleges of this realm have been . . . builded to sustain and keep societies of learned men professing study and prayer, for the edification of the Church of God . . . therefore expressly willeth and commandeth that no manner of person, being either the head or member of any college or cathedral church within this realm, shall . . . have . . . within the precinct of any such college his wife, or other woman, to abide and dwell in the same, or to frequent and haunt any lodging within the same college.

Order of Queen Elizabeth prohibiting the residence of women in colleges, 9 August 1561, in J. Bruce and T. Perowne (eds.), *Correspondence of Matthew Parker*, **1853, p. 146**

The Queen's Injunction brought forth a strong reaction from the clergy. Bishop Cox wrote anxiously to Parker:

1.17

In cathedral churches you know the dean and prebendaries have large and several houses, one distant from another, and if their wives be driven out, I suppose you shall seldom find in most of the churches either dean or prebendary resident there . . . There is but one prebendary continually dwelling with his family in Ely Church. Turn him out, doves and owls may dwell there for any continual housekeeping . . . God mercifully provided for his clergy in Moses's time . . . Nay, God saw that such marriage was natural and, as St Paul says, honourable, and to forbid or deface marriage is the doctrine of devils . . . Albeit of late years, fond [= foolish] and blind devotion in the Latin Church has marvellously [= astonishingly] perverted this godly ordinance with forbidding that which God made free, and with separating of them whom God has joined.

Cox to Parker, August 1561, in J. Bruce and T. Perowne (eds.),
Correspondence of Matthew Parker, **1853, pp. 151–2**

Questions

1   What do you understand by the following:
  (i) 'The prebendaries' [**1.17, line 1**]
  (ii) 'doves and owls may dwell there for any continual housekeeping' [**1.17, lines 6–7**]?
2   Explain Cox's argument in the final sentence of **1.17**.
3   Is the dispute over married clergy [**1.15–1.17**] a sign that Elizabeth remained in some respects a Catholic?
4   Why, in view of documents to **1.15** to **1.17** and in view of other evidence in this chapter, do you think that Elizabeth appointed a married man to be archbishop of Canterbury?

William Cecil wisely followed up Elizabeth's Injunction with a warning letter to Archbishop Parker:

1.18

Your Grace shall understand, that I have hitherto a troublesome progress to stay the Queen's Majesty from daily offence conceived against the clergy, by reason of the undiscreet behaviour of the readers and ministers of these counties of Suffolk and Essex. Surely here be many slender ministers and such nakedness of religion as it   5
overthroweth my credit. Her Majesty continueth very ill affected to the state of matrimony in the clergy. And if I were not therein very stiff, her Majesty would utterly and openly condemn and forbid it . . .
The Bishop of Norwich is blamed even of the best sort for his   10
remissness in ordering his clergy. He winketh at schismatics and anabaptists, as I am informed. Surely I see great variety in ministration. A surplice may not be borne here. And the ministers follow the folly of the people, calling it charity to feed their fond humour. Oh, my Lord, what shall become of this time?   15

Cecil to Parker, 12 August, 1561 in J. Bruce and T. T. Perowne (eds.),
Correspondence of Matthew Parker, **1853, pp. 148–9**

Elizabeth's frustration with the clergy was turned against Archbishop Parker, who bore the brunt of the Queen's anger in a personal meeting. Parker afterwards wrote bitterly to Cecil:

1.19

Horsekeepers' wives, porters', pantlers', and butlers' wives, may have their cradles going, and honest learned men expulsed with open note, who only keep the hospitality, who only be students and preachers, who only be unfeigned orators, in open prayers for the Queen's Majesty's prosperity and continuance; where others say their back   5
pater-nosters in corners . . .
I have neither joy of hours, land or name, so abused by my natural sovereign good lady: for whose service and honour I would not think it cost to spend my life . . . I have, for the execution of her laws and orders, purchased the hatred of the adversaries, and also, for   10
moderating some things indifferent, have procured to have the foul reports of some Protestants.

Parker to Cecil, (not dated) 1561, in J. Bruce and T. Perowne (eds.), *Correspondence of Matthew Parker***, 1853, no. CXIV**

However unreasonable her stand on clerical marriage, Elizabeth had good reason to feel that the bishops were failing to maintain the traditional liturgical standards which she expected. Some of the clergy she had chosen wanted a gradual movement towards the kind of Church they had experienced on the continent, whereas Elizabeth was intent on defending the Settlement achieved in 1559. She was conservative by nature and had no wish to see her Church evolve. A theological foundation for the new Church was provided in 1563, when Parker drew up the Thirty-Nine Articles. These were passed in Convocation and became the basic doctrine of the Church of England. The Settlement was complete, but Elizabeth's religious problems were only just beginning.

Questions

1   What do you understand by the following phrases:
    (i) 'nakedness of religion' [**1.18, line 5**]
    (ii) 'schismatics and anabaptists' [**1.18, lines 11–12**]
    (iii) 'charity to feed their fond humour' [**1.18, lines 14–15**]
    (iv) 'may have their cradles going' [**1.19, lines 1–2**]
    (v) 'unfeigned orators' [**1.19, line 4**]
    (vi) 'their back pater-nosters in corners' [**1.19, lines 5–6**]?

2   Why do you think Parker speaks of having 'procured to have the foul reports of some Protestants' [1.19, lines 11–12]?

3   Of what value are private letters expressing strong emotions to the historian in assessing the character of the writers? What dangers are there in using such letters in building up narrative [1.18 and 1.19]?

4   To what extent do you feel the Settlement of 1559 accurately reflects Elizabeth's religious views?

2 Marriage, the Succession and foreign policy

The problems of marriage and succession were two of the central issues of Tudor foreign policy and Elizabeth was aware, as her predecessors had been, of the dangers of a disputed succession. Nevertheless, she realised that her choice of a husband could also threaten the unity of her realm. To have chosen an English nobleman would have generated faction, while to have chosen a foreign prince might have resulted in England being subordinated to a foreign power, as had happened in the case of her sister, Mary. In 1558 the Spanish ambassador, de Feria, wrote to Philip II:

2.1

> Everybody thinks that she will not marry a foreigner and they cannot
> make out whom she favours, so that nearly every day some new cry is
> raised about a husband. They have dropped the Earls of Arundel and
> Westmoreland and say now that she will marry William Howard's
> son or Pickering . . . They will look with more favour on the   5
> Archduke Ferdinand than on your Majesty, when they have made up
> their mind to accept a foreigner, because they think he will always
> reside in the country, and will have no quarrel with France . . .
>
> **Count de Feria to Philip II, 14 December 1558, in *Calendar of State
> Papers Spanish*, vol. 1, pp. 8–9**

In spite of pressure from foreign princes, Parliament and her own Privy Council, Elizabeth refused to be rushed into marriage. In 1566 she replied to a petition from Parliament:

2.2

> I did send them answer by my Council I would marry (although of
> mine own disposition I was not inclined thereunto) . . . The second
> point was the limitation of the succession of the crown: wherein was
> nothing said for my safety but only for themselves. A strange thing
> that the foot should direct the head in so weighty a cause . . . I am   5
> sure there was not one of them that ever was a second person, as I

have been, and have tasted of the practices against my sister . . . I am
your anointed Queen. I will never be by violence constrained to do
anything . . . Your petition is to deal in the limitation of the
succession. At this present it is not convenient; nor never shall be   10
without some peril unto you and certain danger unto me . . .

Queen Elizabeth to the House of Commons, 1566, in John Neale,
***Elizabeth and her Parliaments*, pp. 147–50**

To Elizabeth the question of who should succeed her was an equally
difficult one, best left unanswered until the pressure on her to do so was
irresistible. And while she refrained from naming her successor she knew
that she could rely on the support of her people, among whom malcontents
would have no obvious rival around whom to organise plots.

However, Elizabeth's Protestant advisers feared that if she died without
heir – and they despaired of her life when she contracted smallpox in 1562
– the throne would go to the young Queen of Scots, widow of the French
King and a Catholic. To them this would have been a disaster, threatening
civil war and subordinating England to the power of France. Elizabeth's
own views on the Queen of Scots were shown in this reply to a suggestion
by the Scottish ambassador that she name Mary Stuart her legal successor:

2.3

I will be Queen of England so long as I live; after my death let them
succeed to whom in right it shall appertain if that be your Queen (as
I know not who should be before her), I will not be against it . . .
you assume . . . that, upon this declaration, the friendship would be
more firm between us. I fear you are deceived; I fear it would be   5
rather an origin of hatred . . .
Is it like that I shall be well pleased in regard of her, with a continual
view of mine own hearse?
. . . I am well acquainted with the nature of this people; I know how
easily they dislike the present state of affairs; I know what nimble   10
eyes they bear to the next succession . . . I have learned this from
experience of mine own times. When my sister Mary was Queen,
what prayers were made by many to see me placed in her seat . . .
Now then, if the affections of our people grow faint . . . what may we
look for when evil-minded men shall have a foreign prince appointed   15
the certain successor to the crown? In how great danger shall I be
. . . when a prince so powerful, so near unto me, shall be declared

my successor? . . . Assuredly, if my successor were known to the world, I would never esteem my state to be safe.

Queen Elizabeth to the House of Commons, 1559, in Sir John Hayward, *Annals*, pp. 78–85

Questions

1   Why do you suppose that in 1558 'everybody thinks . . . [Elizabeth] will not marry a foreigner' [**2.1, line 1**]?

2   What light do documents **2.1** to **2.3** throw on Elizabeth's reasons for remaining unmarried?

3   How would you characterise the *tone* of document **2.2**? What can we learn from that tone?

4   Was it irresponsible of Elizabeth not to settle the question of the succession in the early part of her reign?

Elizabeth's attitude towards Mary Stuart was governed by the desire to avoid making the Queen of Scots a focus for discontent with her rule. While never denying the claims of Mary to succeed her, she studiously avoided naming her directly. Clearly, as an eighteen-year-old widow, Mary would need to re-marry and Elizabeth intended to have a say in who she chose. In 1564 it was suggested that Mary should marry Robert Dudley, Earl of Leicester, but instead she chose Lord Darnley, a man of weak character who proved an unpopular choice in the eyes of the English.

When Mary took the Earl of Bothwell as her lover, and Lord Darnley met his violent end at Kirk-o'-Field, the young Queen of Scots was implicated in her husband's murder. She was driven from Scotland and took refuge in England in 1568. While continuing to view Mary as a fellow monarch, Elizabeth could not conceal her deep concern at the grievous crimes in which Mary seemed to have been involved. This is borne out in the report by Lord Scrope and Sir Francis Knollys of their first meeting with the Queen of Scots:

2.4

We found the Queen of Scots in her chamber of presence[1] ready to receive us . . . After our delivery of your Highness's letters, she fell into some passion with the water in her eyes, and therewith she drew us with her into her bed-chamber, where she complained unto us for that your Highness did not answer her expectation for the admitting   5 her into your presence forthwith, that upon declaration of her

innocence, your Highness would either without delay give her aid
yourself to the subduing of her enemies, or else, being now come of
goodwill and not of necessity . . . your Highness would at the least
forthwith give her passage[2] through your country into France, to seek   10
aid at other princes' hands, not doubting but both the French King
and the King of Spain would give her relief . . . Unto the first part
whereof we answered, that your Highness was inwardly sorry and
very much grieved that you could not do her that great honour to
admit her solemnly and worthily into your presence, by reason of this   15
great slander of murder, whereof she was not yet purged [= cleared].
But we said that we were sure that your Highness's affection towards
her was great.

[1] 'chamber of presence' = room in which a monarch gives audience
[2] 'give her passage' = let her pass

**Lord Scrope and Sir Francis Knollys to Queen Elizabeth, May 1568,
in T. Wright, *Queen Elizabeth and her times*, 1838, vol. 1, pp. 277–9**

In spite of the most urgent advice from Parliament and from her personal
advisers, Elizabeth refused to take action against Mary Stuart, who proved
to be the target for continuous diplomatic intrigue and plots. As the years
passed it became increasingly unlikely that Elizabeth would be able to
provide an heir even if she did marry, and consequently the person of the
Scottish Queen remained inviolable. Yet she was unacceptable to most
English people who preferred the claims of Mary's Protestant son, James.

   In view of the assassination of William of Orange and the abortive
Throckmorton Plot in favour of Mary Stuart in 1584, Burghley and
Walsingham produced the Bond of Association in the same year. It was an
immediate success and galvanised the ruling classes into support for the
Queen. The Bond of Association was an oath, swearing never to accept any
claimant to the throne in whose name an attempt had been made on
Elizabeth's life. It also bound those taking it to hunt such a person to death
– an invitation to lynch law.

   By 1585 Catholic forces in France led by the Duke of Guise were
prepared to support a rebellion in England in favour of Mary Stuart. In fact,
Walsingham's agents had uncovered a whole network of plans and plots
aimed at the overthrow of Elizabeth. In 1584 Francis Throckmorton
declared his treason:

2.5

With a resolute determination agreed on by the Scottish Queen and
her confederates in France . . . and also in England, for the invading

of the realm. That the Duke of Guise should be the principal leader
and executor of that invasion. That the pretension[1] which should be
publicly notified should be to deliver the Scottish Queen to liberty, 5
and to procure, even by force, from the Queen's Majesty a tolerance
in religion for the pretended [= alleged] Catholics; but the intention,
the bottom whereof should not at the first be made known to all men,
should be, upon the Queen's Majesty's resistance, to remove her
Majesty from her crown and state.

[1] 'pretension' = alleged aim

Harleian Miscellany (1808 edn) vol. 1, pp. 525–6

Walsingham had learned of clear Spanish and Papal complicity in the plot,
sufficient for Elizabeth to dismiss Mendoza, the Spanish ambassador, from
her Court. The evidence against Mary Stuart was incontrovertible. As
Spain prepared an expedition which intended to bring to an end Elizabeth's
rule in England, conspirators much nearer home planned immediate
action. In 1586 Mary wrote to Babington:

2.6

Everything being prepared, and the forces as well within as without
. . . then you must set the six gentlemen to work and give order that,
their design accomplished, I may be in some way got away from here
and that all your forces shall be simultaneously in the field to receive
me while we await foreign assistance . . . 5
Now as no certain day can be appointed for the performance of the
said gentlemen's enterprise, I desire them to have always near them,
or at least at Court, four brave men well horsed to advertise speedily
the success of their design, as soon as it is done, to those appointed to
get me away from hence, so as to be able to get here before my 10
keeper is informed of the said execution . . .

**Mary to Babington, 17 July 1586, in A. Labanoff, *Lettres, etc., de
Marie Stuart*, 1852 vol. 6, pp. 385–96**

However, their actions were being closely monitored by Walsingham, and
in 1587 he was able to break the Babington conspiracy and implicate Mary
in plans to have Elizabeth killed. As details of Mary's plots became known it
was decided by the Privy Council that James's claims to the English throne
must be protected from his mother's fall:

2.7

> We the lords and others of her majesty's said Privy Council whose
> names are underwritten do manifest and declare that we had no
> intention in any wise to prejudice the noble Prince James the Sixth,
> now King of Scots, in anything that might touch and concern him in
> house or blood, but to leave him in such and the same state as he   5
> should or might have been if the same sentence and judgement had
> not been had or given, and in no other.

'Intention of the Commissioners for Hearing Mary's Cause',
October 25 1586, in *Calendar of State Papers Scottish*, vol. 9, p. 108

By 1587 Elizabeth was certain of Mary's guilt but could not bring herself to
condemn a fellow monarch. She wavered between concepts of public and
private morality, even indirectly asking Mary's keeper, the upright
Puritan, Sir Amyas Paulet, as a signatory of the Bond of Association, to
relieve her of the difficulty of acting herself by quietly disposing of her rival.
In the event, the Privy Council induced Elizabeth to sign Mary's death
warrant, although after it was put into effect she bitterly recriminated
against them and threatened them with death or at least dismissal.

   James VI of Scotland made only a token protest at the execution of his
mother and though Elizabeth was still not prepared to recognise him
officially as her successor, she was not prepared to allow anyone to speak
against him. In the last days of Elizabeth's life Robert Cecil began a secret
correspondence with James, in order to smooth his accession to power:

2.8

> Your best approach towards your greatest end, is by your Majesty's
> clear and temperate courses to secure the heart of the highest, to
> whose sex and quality [= status] nothing is so improper as either
> needless expostulations, or overmuch curiosity in her own actions.
> The first showing unquietness [= anxiety] in yourself, the second   5
> challenging [= pursuing] some untimely interest in hers; both which,
> as they are best forborne when there is no cause, so be it far from me
> . . . to persuade you to receive wrong and be silent . . . Although it
> be a common rule with many rising princes to refuse no address, yet
> you will find it in your case, that a choice election of a few in the   10
> present will be of more use than any general acclamation of many.

Robert Cecil to James VI, 1601, in *Correspondence of James VI and*
***Robert Cecil*, Camden Society, 1861, pp. 16–18**

It was only at the very end that Elizabeth finally named her successor: 'I will that a king succeed me and who but my kinsman the king of Scots'.

Questions

1   Was Elizabeth's response to Mary's arrival in England [2.4] a sensible one?
2   If Mary were not assisted by Elizabeth, what would the dangers to England have been [2.4]?
3   What considerations might have held Elizabeth back from executing Mary following revelations such as those in 2.5 and 2.6?
4   Why, in view of 2.7 and 2.8, do you suppose that Elizabeth could not be brought to declare James her heir until her deathbed?
5   Explain, and consider the soundness of, the advice Robert Cecil gave to James VI in the last sentence of document 2.8.

Anglo-Spanish relations, 1558–85

The first decade of Elizabeth's reign marked a gradual weakening of the traditional Anglo-Burgundian alliance of her predecessors. This was not the result of deliberate policy on the part of either Elizabeth or Philip of Spain. In fact, Philip preferred to see the heretic Elizabeth on the throne of England than the pro-French Mary Stuart, and twice persuaded the Pope not to excommunicate her. However, Elizabeth's assertion of independence and her desire that England should no longer be 'a bone between two dogs' made it likely that she would eventually clash with Spain, particularly over the Netherlands and the activities of English mariners in Spanish waters.

A cumulative deterioration of relations finally provoked a crisis in Anglo-Spanish relations in 1568. Most importantly the success of the Duke of Alva's forces in the Netherlands threatened Elizabeth by placing a powerful military presence on the western littoral of the continent opposite England. By 1568 the Duke of Alva had assembled a huge army of 50,000 in the Netherlands, just thirty miles from the coast of Kent. William Cecil was alarmed at what the Spanish commander might do once the Netherlands had been subdued. England was militarily impotent against such a threat.

While Elizabeth was no supporter of the rebels in the Netherlands she appreciated the danger posed by Alva. Consequently, Elizabeth resorted to a policy of harassment, supporting privateers like La Marck and his 'Sea Beggars' and letting them use English harbours. She encouraged English mariners like John Hawkins to break into the trade with West Africa and Spanish America, ventures which she backed financially along with her

Court officials. Philip reacted to English provocation by dismissing Elizabeth's ambassador in Spain, Dr John Mann, for calling the Pope 'a canting little monk'. He replaced the popular ambassador to England, Guzman de Silva, with the inept Guerau de Spes, who merely intensified the developing rift.

As an ambassador, de Spes found it very difficult to make useful contacts at Court and became increasingly dependent for his information on rumours and the embittered views of malcontents. This is how he described the leading figures in Elizabeth's government:

2.9

> The principal person in the Council at present is William Cecil . . . He is a man of mean sort, but very astute, false, lying, and full of artifice. He is a great heretic, and such a clownish Englishman as to believe that all the Christian princes joined together are not able to injure the sovereign of his country, and he therefore treats their   5
> ministers with great arrogance.
> This man manages the bulk of the business, and by means of his vigilance and craftiness, together with his utter unscrupulousness of word and deed, thinks to outwit the ministers of other princes. This to a certain extent he has hitherto succeeded in doing. Next after   10
> him, the man who has most to do with affairs is Robert Dudley, Earl of Leicester, not that he is fit for such work, but because of the great favour with which the Queen regards him. He is a light and greedy man who maintains the robbers and lives by their plunder . . . The other man who has his hand in the government is the Lord Keeper of   15
> the Great Seal. He is an obstinate and most malignant heretic, and, being Cecil's brother-in-law, always agrees with him. The Admiral does not interfere very much in arranging matters, but he is a very shameless thief without any religion at all, which latter also may be said of the Earl of Sussex . . . The Earl of Bedford also belongs to   20
> the Council. In person and manners he is a monstrosity and a great heretic. There are others of less authority than these men, lawyers, creatures of Cecil who only repeat what he says.

> **Guerau de Spes to Philip II, 1565, in *Calendar of State Papers Spanish*, Eliz. II, 364**

The incident which provoked the crisis of 1568 was the seizure by Elizabeth of Spanish bullion ships which had been blown into an English port while carrying Genoese gold to pay Alva's troops in the Netherlands, Alva responded by seizing all English merchants and their property in Antwerp. Again, the crisis was fanned into flame by de Spes, who wrote to advise Alva:

2.10

> Cecil was very grave about it, as also was the earl of Leicester. Sometimes they said they were guarding it for his Majesty, and sometimes that it belonged to other persons; but they would not say whether they had sent similar orders to Plymouth and Falmouth. Their refusal to declare themselves on this point, however, proves   5
> that they have done so. They consulted the Queen and then said that the money was in safe keeping and no other answer could then be given. I pressed for an audience and they told me to ask again after dinner, they in the meantime being closeted with the ambassador of the prince of Conde, so that I could get no reply from them . . . The   10
> affair is thus in a very bad way and these people are determined to do any wickedness, so this money will not be recovered. I pray Your Excellency do not fail to seize all English property and send word to Spain instantly for them to do the same there.
>
> **Guerau de Spes to the Duke of Alva, 22 December 1568, in *Calendar of State Papers Spanish*, 1568–79, p. 91**

Cecil was clearly behind the plan to seize the Genoese gold but neither he nor his mistress expected Spain to react so violently.

2.11

> Her Majesty has heard that the Duke of Alva, governor of the States of Flanders for her brother the King of Spain, had suddenly ordered the detention of all merchants and other subjects of Her Majesty in the city of Antwerp, and had placed guards of soldiers over them, and had sequestrated all their property . . . which is a strange and   5
> unheard of thing for the house of Burgundy to do the Crown of England . . . her Majesty thinks fit to declare briefly the facts of the case . . .
> An officer of Her Majesty in a port in the west part of England advised the arrival from Spain of three or four small boats called   10

cutters bringing a quantity of money belonging to certain Italian
merchants . . . on the coast there were many armed French ships of
war on the watch for these cutters . . . The Spanish ambassador . . .
asked that . . . orders should be given for the defence of these vessels
and the treasure against the French . . . At this time the Queen learnt 15
that the money was the property of certain merchants and decided
that it was not unreasonable nor opposed to the *bonos mores* of
sovereigns in their own country that . . . she should negotiate with
the owners thereof with their full consent . . . for borrowing from
them all or part of it . . . 20
Before she saw the ambassador . . . she learned that all the ships,
goods and merchandize of her subjects were embargoed and seized in
Antwerp on the 29th December.

**Proclamation of Queen Elizabeth 'Respecting the Detention of the
Money being sent to Spain', 1568, in *Calendar of State Papers
Spanish*, vol. 2, pp. 99–101**

By 1572 Anglo-Spanish relations began to improve and the Netherlands
trade resumed after the years of crisis. Spain was fully committed in the
Netherlands and in the Mediterranean and wished to reach an agreement
with England. Elizabeth reciprocated by removing her support for English
privateers in South American waters and by expelling the Sea Beggars
from English ports. However, this proved to be an unwelcome concession
to the Spanish for La Marck immediately captured the port of Brill and
thereby raised the banner of revolt in the Netherlands again.

Elizabeth's policy on the Dutch revolt was clear: she wanted Philip of
Spain to remove his army and to restore autonomy to the provinces as in
his father, Charles V's, time. However, she recognised the danger to
English interests of France expanding into the Netherlands and sought
every means to prevent this. In 1575 Sir Henry Cobham was sent to Spain
to negotiate with Philip II. Among his instructions from the Queen were
the following points:

2.12

3   After this he shall show the King that however he has been
informed of her doings with his subjects in the Low Countries, if he
knew how often and earnestly she has been solicited to take
possession of Holland and Zealand he might say that he never had
such a friend as she has been. If some speedy remedy be not taken 5

those countries will be at the devotion of the French King, who and
his predecessor have continually aided the Prince of Orange with
money to maintain his wars, and now continues the same with a
monthly secret pay. As nothing could be so hurtful to the King and
dangerous to herself as this, she earnestly requires him to divert his   10
course now in hand by allowing his subjects to enjoy their ancient
privileges, and suffering them to live freely from the extremities of
the Inquisition. In this behalf he is to say that she will be content
to use any office of mediation for the compounding of these
differences . . .   15

4   Touching the removing of strangers out of the country, as the
Prince and his confederates give out that the ancient privileges
require, to the due observation of which the King is sworn, she
cannot see how the king in honour can well deny it; but howsoever it
be, he should consider that the greatest monarchs have been driven to 20
yield sundry times to necessity, and that the French King being so
puissant a Prince it stands him to yield, rather than lose a country so
well worth keeping. In case her good brother will not allow of these
her friendly advertisements . . . he is to signify that . . . she may be
found for her own safety to be a dealer therein . . . to preserve her   25
own realm rather than from a desire to invade anything belonging to
him.

**Instructions to Sir Henry Cobham sent into Spain by the Queen,
1 July 1575, in *Calendar of State Papers Foreign*, 1575–7, pp. 76–7**

The sack of Antwerp in 1576 by mutinous Spanish troops undermined
Elizabeth's policy of neutrality towards the rebels in the Netherlands. With
her Council divided, and zealots such as Walsingham and Leicester urging
her to intervene militarily and to accept the Dutch offer of sovereignty over
the Netherlands, she found it increasingly difficult to reject their
arguments. Spain's new ambassador, Bernardino de Mendoza, the
shrewdest of all Philip II's representatives at Elizabeth's Court, commented
as follows:

2.13

During the few days I have been here and in my conversation with
the Queen I have found her much opposed to your Majesty's
interests . . . and most of her ministers are quite alienated from us,

particularly those who are most important, as, although there are
seventeen Councillors, with the two secretaries, Hatton and the new   5
ones, the bulk of the business depends upon the Queen, Leicester,
Walsingham and Cecil, the latter of whom, although he takes part in
the resolution of them by virtue of his office, absents himself on
many occasions, as he is opposed to the Queen's helping the rebels so
effectively and thus weakening her own position. He does not wish to   10
break with Leicester and Walsingham on the matter, they being very
much wedded to the States . . . They urge the business under cloak
of preserving their religion, which Cecil cannot well oppose . . . Some
of the Councillors are well disposed to your Majesty but Leicester,
whose spirit is Walsingham, is so highly favoured by the Queen,   15
notwithstanding his bad character, that he centres in his hands . . .
most of the business of the country.

**Mendoza to Philip II, March 1578, in *Calendar of State Papers
Spanish*, 1568–79, p. 572**

Questions

1   How useful to Philip II do you suppose ambassadorial reports like
     2.9 and **2.10** were?
2   Would you agree that Spain overreacted [**2.11**] to Elizabeth's actions
     as described in **2.10**?
3   Do documents **2.12** and **2.13** suggest that Elizabeth was reluctant to
     fight Spain, or simply waiting for the right moment to do so?
4   Do documents **2.9** to **2.13** suggest that Anglo–Spanish relations were
     dominated by religious considerations?

Spanish power waxed during the period 1579–81 when Philip II was able
to take the throne of Portugal and add its considerable wealth to his own.
In addition he gained the powerful Portuguese navy which meant that
now he could challenge the English at sea. Elizabeth was forced to adopt
more overtly anti-Spanish activities, notably in welcoming the Portuguese
Pretender to her court, subsidising the Duke of Anjou and his forces in the
Netherlands and knighting Sir Francis Drake in public, thereby condoning
his predatory raids on Spanish commerce.

The death of Anjou and William of Orange within months in 1584
seriously weakened England's position. It seemed that nothing could now
prevent a complete collapse of the Netherlands revolt. In France the
Protestant leader, Henry of Navarre, was now heir to the throne and this
resulted in the creation of the Catholic League under the Guise family. By

the Treaty of Joinville in 1584 the Catholic League received the backing of the King of Spain. No longer could Elizabeth look to France to block Spanish expansion. The assassination of the great Protestant leader William of Orange came as a great blow to the Protestant cause throughout Europe. Dutch ambassadors pressed Elizabeth once more to accept the sovereignty of the Netherlands, but her reluctance is made clear by Burghley in the following extract:

2.14

> Her Highness cannot be induced by any writing or harangue you can
> make to accept the principality or proprietorship as sovereign, and it
> will therefore be labour lost for you to exhibit any writing for the
> purpose of changing her intention. It will be better to content
> yourself with her Majesty's consent to assist you and to take you   5
> under her protection.
>
> **Burghley, from a Dutch account of the interview, in J. L. Motley,**
> ***The Rise of the Dutch Republic***, **1855, vol. 1, p. 321**

Reluctant as she was to intervene directly Elizabeth now knew that only military intervention in the Netherlands would prevent a total Spanish triumph. At the Treaty of Nonsuch in 1585 she agreed:

2.15

> 1   That the Queen of England should send to the United Provinces
> an aid of . . . 5,000 footmen and one thousand horse, under the
> conduct of a Governor-General who should be a person of quality
> and rank, well-affected to the true religion, and under other good
> chiefs and captains, all of whom shall be paid by the Queen as long   5
> as the war lasts.
>
> 2   The United Provinces, individually and collectively, bind
> themselves, when, by God's grace and her Majesty's assistance, they
> shall be re-established in peace and repose, to repay all that her
> Majesty shall have disbursed, as well for the levy of the troops and   10
> their transportation, as for their wages . . .
>
> 3   For greater assurance of the repayment the town of Flushing, the
> castle of Rammekens, in the isle of Walcheren, and the town of Brill,

with two fortresses in Holland shall within one month of the
confirmation of the Contract be placed in the hands of such   15
governors as it shall please her Majesty to appoint . . . until [she]
shall be completely repaid . . .

The Treaty with the United Provinces, 10 August 1585 in J. Dumont,
Corps universal diplomatique, **1728, vol 5, pp. 454–5**

War was now certain, yet it was a war that Elizabeth had not sought. Even
as Drake set out to 'singe the king of Spain's beard' by attacking Spanish
ports, Elizabeth was pursuing peace with the Duke of Parma. In December
1587 she advised her peace commissioners:

2.16

You may then declare 'that the causes now to be treated upon
concern on the one part personally the King of Spain and us'; that
the former leagues and intercourse may be revived and our dominions
and people be again as they were before any arrests were made of
their persons and goods on either side, which chiefly began in the   5
time of the Duke of Alva. And on the other hand it is to be specially
considered how to establish the Low Countries in peace and lawful
government by natural born subjects as in former times, without
opposition by Spaniards and strangers, by whose hostile actions has
been overthrown all good intercourse of the subjects and liberty for   10
merchants . . .

Instructions for the peace commissioners sent to the Duke of Parma,
December 1587, in *Calendar of State Papers Foreign,* **1587, p. 475**

With the Spanish Armada approaching completion there was never any
hope of peace, as Parma wrote to Philip II:

2.17

The peace negotiations with the English have ended in the recall of
the Commissioners by the Queen, and they have departed by way of
Calais. My efforts to induce them to continue the negotiations,
notwithstanding the presence of the Armada, were unavailing.

Parma to Philip II, 28 July 1588, in *Calendar of State Papers*
Spanish, **vol. 4, p. 366**

Questions

1   Why did Elizabeth refuse to become Queen of the Netherlands
    [2.14], but send Leicester over with an army of 6,000 men [2.15]?
2   Explain why England was so concerned about the fate of the
    Netherlands.
3   Elizabeth's policy towards Spain has been described by some modern
    historians as 'indecisive and ineffective' and 'too little too late'. How
    far can documents **2.14** to **2.17** be used to support these judgments?

Anglo-French relations 1558–85

Elizabeth had inherited a realm militarily weak and vulnerable to attack
from both France and Scotland. The loss of Calais in the last days of Mary's
reign had given France control of the entire southern wind-ward coast of
the Channel, which in the days of sail meant that an invasion fleet from
French ports might find their English adversaries pinned in harbour by
adverse winds. In Scotland the young Mary Stuart, wife of the Dauphin
Francis, declared herself legitimate Catholic claimant to the English
throne. With the French strongly entrenched in Scotland it was more
important than ever that Elizabeth maintained the Spanish alliance.
However, unlike her principal advisers Elizabeth was unwilling to
countenance sending troops to aid the Protestant rebels against the Queen
of Scots. As she was to maintain throughout her reign, 'It is against God's
law to aid any subjects against their natural prince'.

The death of Henry II in 1559 brought Mary Stuart to the throne of
France. It also brought her under the influence of her Guise relations, Duke
Francis and the Cardinal of Lorraine, who were determined to stamp out
the revolt of the Lords of the Congregation in Scotland, as well as assert
Mary's claims to the English throne. Elizabeth could not now avoid taking
action and English troops were eventually sent into Scotland where they
forced the French garrison at Leith to negotiate. In the Treaty of
Edinburgh, 6 July 1560, English and French troops were withdrawn from
Scotland and Mary Stuart was forced to renounce her use of the arms and
title of England.

In 1562 civil war broke out in France between the Catholics, led by the
Guise family, and the Protestant Huguenots. For the next thirty years these
wars of religion were to dominate French history and to influence Anglo-
French relations. Cecil's aggressive policy had proved successful in
Scotland and when the Huguenots in France called on Elizabeth for
assistance she showed none of her usual caution. Eager to regain Calais,
Elizabeth found her Council united in supporting military intervention in

France. The resultant fiasco, in which the Huguenots patched up their quarrel with the Guises and turned on the English at Le Havre taught Elizabeth the valuable lesson that national security was of far greater value than foreign adventures.

After 1564, Catherine de Medici ruled in France as regent for her young son, Charles IX, and maintained peace both at home and abroad. She was unsympathetic both to Mary Stuart and to the Guises, and through her friendship Elizabeth managed to remove the two main threats to her realm which had existed in 1558. However, England's rift with Spain in 1568 and the arrival of the Queen of Scots as a refugee, combined to trigger off the rising of the Northern Earls in 1569. Although the Earl of Sussex was able to disperse the rebels, many crossed the border into Scotland and joined supporters of Mary Stuart there. These latter looked to France for assistance and though Elizabeth was unprepared to intervene directly she advised Sussex that if he found it necessary to cross into Scotland she would not be displeased if he supported the forces of the boy King, James VI, against those of his mother, Mary Stuart:

2.18

> If any of them who shall proclaim the Queen [Mary Stuart] shall be of those who have aided, or do aid her [Elizabeth's] rebels, or have invaded her country, he shall proceed against them as against her enemies, and if they reply by moving [= urging] him to open [= declare] himself plainly for defence of the King's title, and   5
> suppressing the Queen, he may say that he has 'commission to deal with persons and not with titles', and he has charge to aid the persons who are her friends, and who also profess the King's authority.

Elizabeth to the Earl of Sussex, 30 April 1570, in *Calendar of State Papers Scottish*, vol. 3, p. 139

Aware of the continuing danger of French influence in Scotland, Elizabeth at last intervened militarily to support the Anglophile regent, the Earl of Morton. Having assisted Morton to restore order in Scotland, Elizabeth promptly withdrew any further aid for fear of alienating France. Unlike her Tudor predecessors, notably her father, she had no interest in trying to absorb Scotland into her realm.

In the late 1560s Huguenot volunteers from France were fighting in the Netherlands against the Duke of Alva. Protestant zealots on Elizabeth's Council, like Walsingham and Leicester, favoured the idea of a Protestant

League against Spain. However, they were strongly opposed by Cecil and Sussex, who feared a French presence in the Low Countries as much as they feared a Spanish one. Cecil's arguments were contained in this 'Memorial' and Elizabeth found the arguments convincing:

2.19

> If . . . the Duke of Alva is sufficiently . . . able to resist all attempts, so as he may detain his master's countries from the conquest of the French, then it is like to be best for England to let both sides alone for a time, otherwise the French may be offended and the Spaniard not made sure, and if they accord we shall be sure of neither.   5
>
> If . . . the French begin to possess any part of . . . the maritime parts, then it is like that the French . . . may be too potent neighbours for us and therefore [it] may be good for us to use all the means . . . to stay that course.
>
> If the French proceed to possess the maritime coasts and frontiers   10 it seemeth to be good that . . . the Duke of Alva were informed secretly of the Queen's Majesty's disposition to assist the king his master by all honourable means she might in the defence of his inheritance, so as it may appear to her that he will discharge his subjects of their intolerable oppression, restore them to their ancient   15 liberties, reconcile his nobility to him, deliver them from the fear of the Inquisition and continue with her Majesty the ancient league for amity and traffic in as ample sort as any others, dukes of Burgundy, heretofore have done.

'Memorial for Matters of Flanders', Burghley, June 1572, in C. Read,
Lord Burghley and Queen Elizabeth, p. 74

Questions

1   Is document **2.18** consistent with Elizabeth's earlier assertion (p. 49) that 'it is against God's Law to aid any subject against their natural prince'?
2   Consider document **2.19** in the light of your conclusions about the previous section of this chapter.
3   Does document **2.19** demonstrate that Burghley was more pro-Spanish than anti-Spanish?

The rift with Spain made a French match more attractive. In order to secure French support against the Duke of Alva in the Netherlands,

Elizabeth began negotiations for marriage to the unattractive and unprepossessing Duke of Alençon. The courtship produced the Treaty of Blois in 1572, but no marriage. In the event the massacre of St Bartholomew's Day prevented further Huguenot involvement in the Netherlands.

It was not until 1578 that France was again able to offer help to the Dutch rebels under William of Orange. Francis, Duke of Alençon (who had now become Duke of Anjou), agreed to send troops independently of his brother, Henry III of France. The forty-five year-old Elizabeth decided to use her strongest diplomatic weapon to lure Anjou into conforming with English policy: she offered him marriage. Piqued by the marriage of her favourite, Robert Dudley, to Lettice Knollys, Elizabeth pursued Anjou with genuine excitement. The proposed marriage divided her Council. The Earl of Sussex gave his thoughts on the alliance with the house of France in this letter to the Queen:

2.20

You shall be assured, by yourself and your husband, to have such a party in France as the French King shall not be able, nor shall not dare, to attempt directly or indirectly anything against you. You shall . . . be able to assure the Protestants of France from peril of massacre by the Papists, and the King from any perilous action by them . . .   5 You shall take away, and suppress, all practise for competition [for the succession to the Crown of England], for Popery, or any other seditious cause, at home or abroad . . . You shall also . . . be able to compel the King of Spain to take reasonable conditions of his subjects in the Low Countries . . .

Earl of Sussex to Elizabeth, in E. Lodge, *Illustrations of British History in the Reign of Elizabeth*, 1838, vol. 2, pp. 109–11

Burghley reflected some of the opposition to the marriage in this Memorandum of 27 March 1579:

2.21

The apparent reasons to dissuade her Majesty from this marriage:

1   It seemeth that her Majesty's years, being about [45] years, may yield occasion to doubt either to her conception or her good delivery; and if she should marry and not conceive then her Majesty would be

discomfited, her realm not provided of a child to be her successor,   5
and yet the realm charged with her husband during her life . . .

4   Finally, doubt may be made that the duke of Alençon, finding
lack of issue by the Queen's Majesty, whereby he shall lack
commodity to enjoy the realm after the Queen's death . . . will have a
purpose to marry with the Queen of Scots, by whom he may hope to   10
enjoy both England and Scotland . . . no nation can be more misliked
than a prince of France . . . because in this age it is seen that all the
Kings of France . . . have governed the realm of France with great
infelicity and namely have sought by all means, both bloody and
otherwise, to extinct the new profession of Christ's gospel . . .

**Burghley, Memorandum on the Alençon Marriage, 27 March 1579, in
C. Read,** *Lord Burghley and Queen Elizabeth***, pp. 208–9**

The extraordinary courtship provoked violent reactions throughout
Elizabethan England. The Puritans were particularly incensed at the
thought of a Catholic consort for Elizabeth and, in 1579, John Stubbs, the
brother-in-law of Thomas Cartwright, attacked the marriage in his book,
The Discovery of a Gaping Gulf. Elizabeth's reaction was as extreme as any of
her reign as the contemporary historian, William Camden, describes:

2.22

She was also much incensed at a book which was written and
published against the marriage in a smart [= sharp] and stinging
style (out of a fear lest religion should be changed) entitled *The gulf
wherein England will be swallowed by the French marriage.* In which
book those of the Council who favoured the marriage are taxed   5
[= attacked] as ungrateful to their prince and country; the Queen
herself (in the midst of several flattering expressions) is glanced at[1] as
unlike herself; the Duke of Anjou slandered with unworthy
reproaches; the French nation odiously defamed; and the marriage
itself, in regard to the difference of religion (as of the daughter of   10
God with a son of Antichrist), with virulent words condemned as
profane, dangerous to the Church and destructive to the
commonwealth . . . John Stubbs . . . the author of this book, William
Page, who dispersed the copies, and Singleton, the printer, were
apprehended . . . Stubbs and Page had their right hands cut off by a   15
cleaver driven through the wrist by the force of a mallet, upon a

scaffold in the market place at Westminster. The printer was
pardoned . . . The multitude was deeply silent, either out of an
horror at this new and unwonted [= unaccustomed] kind of
punishment, or else out of commiseration towards the man, as being   20
of an honest and unblamable repute, or else out of hatred of the
marriage.

¹'glanced at' = criticised obliquely

**W. Camden, *The History of the Most Renowned and Victorious
Princess Elizabeth, late Queen of England*, 1625, pp. 269–70**

Elizabeth was forced to react to the growing power of Philip II and was
prepared to consider an Anglo-French league against Spain. Though the
proposed marriage to Anjou had proved unworkable she sent Walsingham
to France to offer secret aid for Anjou's expedition into the Netherlands.
Walsingham reported the difficulties he faced:

2.23

The principal cause why I was sent over, as I conceived it, and as I
trust your Majesty can call it to remembrance, was to procure a
straighter [= closer] degree of amity [= friendship] between the King
and you, without marriage, and yet to carry myself in the procuring
thereof as might not altogether break off the matter of marriage . . . I   5
cannot but let your Majesty understand, as I declared to you before
my departure, that if your Majesty shall be content to yield to
marriage, I am fully persuaded that the King will be induced to
covenant with you, that you shall be discharged of such burden as the
war may cast upon you . . . All hope to procure the league without   10
marriage is excluded.

**Sir Francis Walsingham to Elizabeth, 16 August 1581, in D. Digges,
*The Compleat Ambassador . . . comprised in letters . . . of Sir
Francis Walsingham*, 1655, p. 291**

Henry III mistrusted Elizabeth's motives and was only prepared to consider
the league against Spain if the marriage with Anjou cemented Anglo-
French relations. This Elizabeth could not agree to and so the league
foundered. However, Elizabeth did finance Anjou herself to the extent of
£60,000 in 1581–2. Anjou's failure and the refusal of Henry III to aid the
Dutch rebels marked an end to Elizabeth's attempts to avoid direct
involvement in the Netherlands.

Questions

1   Do you find the arguments in document **2.20** or **2.21** the more convincing?
2   From what you have discovered about her character so far in this book, would you describe Elizabeth's reaction to John Stubbs' book [**2.22**] as characteristic or not?
3   What might have made the French so insistent on a marriage treaty or no treaty at all in 1581 [**2.23**]?

War 1585–1603

There was no formal declaration of war against Spain in 1585. Leicester's expedition to the Netherlands and Drake's raids were acts of war in their own right even though Elizabeth continued to see the war as merely an extension of her diplomacy. Thus she placed severe restrictions on her commanders, intending Leicester's army only as a way of preventing Parma's total success. When Leicester accepted the title of Governor-General of the Netherlands she was furious with him, believing he was trying to commit her further than she wanted. Sir Thomas Shirley wrote to Leicester, describing Elizabeth's reaction:

2.24

[Her Majesty] used most bitter words against your lordship for your receiving that government, affirming that she did expressly [= explicitly] forbid it unto your lordship in the presence and hearing of divers of her council. I alleged the necessity of it, and your lordship's intent to do all for the best of her Majesty's service; and I   5
told her how those countries did expect you as a governor at your first landing, and that the States[1] dared do no other but to satisfy the people also with that opinion . . . And that, by this means, her Majesty should have the command both of their money, ships and town . . . But all my speech was in vain, for she persisted, saying that   10
your lordship's proceeding was sufficient to make her infamous to all princes, having protested[2] the contrary in a book which is translated into divers and sundry languages.

[1] 'the States' = the Dutch legislative assembly
[2] 'protested' = publicly asserted

Sir Thomas Shirley to Leicester, 14 March 1586, in *Leicester Correspondence*, Camden Society, 1844, p. 172

On the other hand Philip of Spain saw the true significance of English intervention. He knew that the arrival of Leicester in the Netherlands had boosted Dutch hopes at a time when he had thought them beaten, while English mariners were exposing the weaknesses of his colonial system. In fact, the maritime threat from Drake weighed as heavily in Spanish minds as the situation in the Netherlands:

2.25

The intervention of the English in Holland and Zeeland, together with their infestation of the Indies and the Ocean, is of such a nature that defensive methods are not enough to cover everything, but forces us to apply the fire in their homeland, and so fiercely that they will have to rush back and retire from elsewhere . . . They are powerful at   5 sea, and that is their great asset; therefore His Majesty's Armada should not sail under-strength but should be the largest and most powerful one possible . . . For the objective of this Armada is no less the security of the Indies than the recovery of the Netherlands.

Medina Sidonia to Idiaquez, 22 February 1587, in J. Lynch, *Spain under the Habsburgs*, 1964, p. 315

Philip II had no idea of conquering England and multiplying the problems he was already facing in the Netherlands. Instead, he intended his Armada to clear the Channel of English ships and thereby allow Parma, who was in Ghent, to land in Kent and perhaps secure London, before negotiating a general settlement. Parma was far from confident:

2.26

It may be that God desires to punish us for our sins by some heavy disaster. Even if the Armada supplies us with the 6,000 Spaniards as agreed – and they are the sinews of the undertaking – I shall still have too few troops, as the men here are dwindling daily. If I set foot on shore, it will be necessary for us to fight battle after battle. I shall,   5 of course, lose men by wounds and sickness. I must leave the port and town garrisons strongly defended, to keep open my lines of communication: and in a very short time my force will thus be so much reduced as to be quite inadequate to cope with the great multitude of enemies.

Parma to Philip II, 10 March 1588 in *Calendar of State Papers Spanish*, vol. 4, pp. 237–8

The Venetian ambassador in France gave the view of a neutral on the likely success of the Armada:

2.27

It is generally held that the King of Spain will not undertake so vast an enterprise . . . for he . . . knows how much consideration ought to be paid to such a fleet as the English fleet, both on account of its size, and also because the English are men of another mettle from the Spaniards, and enjoy the reputation of being above all the Western nations, expert and active in all naval operations, and great sea-dogs.

Mocenigo to the Doge and Senate of Venice, 29 March 1558, in *Calendar of State Papers Venetian*, vol. 8, p. 349

Questions

1   Comment on the description of Elizabeth's mood in **2.24**. How far does it confirm or differ from the impression of her and you have gained from other material in this book (or elsewhere)?
2   What light do documents **2.25** to **2.27** throw on the failure of the Armada sent against England in 1588?
3   Comment on Medina Sidonia's statement [**2.25, lines 8–9**] that 'the objective of the Armada is no less the security of the Indies than the recovery of the Netherlands.'

Elizabeth's refusal to follow up the defeat of the Armada has been interpreted in many ways. Her defensive strategy frustrated her captains. The failure of Drake's expedition to Portugal in 1589 indicated her inability to control the execution of wartime policy. Yet Elizabeth was aware of her realm's financial and military weakness and never intended to destroy Spain's power or seize her colonial empire, as the younger generation of her advisers wanted. Raleigh spoke of beating 'that great empire in pieces and [making] their kings kings of figs and oranges as in old times'. But Elizabeth knew that England's security rested on the survival of both a powerful Spain and a powerful France, which would counter-balance each other.

At sea Elizabeth's ships tried to disrupt Spanish trade and communications with the Netherlands to win for that country a favourable settlement. Two further Armadas were launched from Spain, though both failed to reach the Channel. For the English the war took on a privateering appearance and the great Cadiz expedition of 1596 was itself a semi-commercial venture, with its effects felt most by Spain's ailing economy.

2.28

> The Spaniards having fresh in memory the great blow received at Cadiz which doth yet represent a fearful object to their eyes; and would have been the utter ruin of his greatness if the English had held it; or if they had stayed but some few days to have intercepted the Indian fleet they had at least clipped his feathers, as manifestly   5
> appeareth by this that, howbeit his fleet came safely into Spain, yet he was forced by his loss at Cadiz and other expenses above his revenues to retain particular men's monies, which hath caused these disorders amongst the merchants throughout Italy and diminished his own credit, as neither in Naples, Genoa or Milan he cannot find any   10
> that for his service will disburse a penny . . . The King is likewise behind with the merchants of Genoa 600,000 crowns.

Guicciardini to Essex, 12 March 1597, Hatfield MSS, VII, pp. 109–110

For eighteen years England maintained troops in the Netherlands and between 1589 and 1596 expeditions were sent to France to support Henry IV against the Spanish. Nevertheless, Elizabeth found the French King a frustrating ally.

2.29

> Sir Edmund Yorke is to be sent to the French King to treat for the sending of English forces to Brittany. He is instructed when he shall have audience with the King to say her Majesty thinks it strange that in the four months since the Spaniards have invaded Brittany, she has not received any knowledge from him of what he means to do for   5
> the repelling of these forces . . . her Majesty is very mindful, first for the loss of so rich a dominion as Brittany, and by consequence of the evil neighbourhood of so mighty a Prince possessing so great enmity towards her . . . Sir Edmund Yorke is now to procure . . . for our

shipping and people the use of the haven of Brest, the commodity of 10
the roads for the ships, and the town and lodgings for the men,
without this assurance neither ship nor men can be in any safety.

**Sir Edmund Yorke sent to the French King, 30 January 1591, in G. B.
Harrison (ed.),** *An Elizabethan Journal,* **pp. 7–8**

Henry IV told Elizabeth that he was not prepared to be anybody's fool, to
'make wars against the King of Spain, that [she] might look out at the
window . . . and behold the tragedies between him and his enemies'. If the
English wanted a port they should win it:

2.30

Considering the humours of some of his Catholic councillors, he
[Henry IV] could not assent to yielding Brest or St. Malo in
particular, but would conclude that the first port town to be taken
from the enemy should be delivered to Her Majesty for the retreat of
her people. He hoped the Queen would not now forsake him, 5
knowing how far she was interested in the common cause. He knew
well what would immediately result for England if the Spanish King
became King of France . . . He also knew how much it would import
her to have so evil a neighbour as the Spaniard in Brittany . . .

From R. B. Wernham (ed.), *List and Analysis of State Papers,
Foreign Series, Elizabeth I,* **vol. 3, June 1591 – April 1592, p. 380**

When in 1595 rebellion broke out in Ireland, the rebel leaders, Tyrone and
O'Donnell, immediately appealed to Spain for help:

2.31

Our only hope of re-establishing the Catholic religion rests on your
assistance. Now or never our Church must be succoured. By the
timidity or negligence of the messengers our former letters have not
reached you. We therefore again beseech you to send us 2,000 or
3,000 soldiers, with money and arms . . . With such aid we hope to 5
restore the faith of the Church, and to secure you a kingdom.

Tyrone and O'Donnell to Philip II, 27 September 1595, in *Calendar
of the Carew MSS,* **ed. J. S. Brewer and W. Bullen, (1867–70), vol. 3,
p. 122**

Elizabeth was forced to virtually bankrupt the country to regain control. In 1599 the Earl of Essex was sent to Ireland as Lord Deputy with an army of 17,000 men but failed to satisfy Elizabeth's demands for outright victory over the rebels. Many of his actions were open to criticism:

2.32

> There hath been idly spent near about a million of Her Majesty's treasure from time to time by the Deputies here, only in making roads and journeys into the north part of Ireland, not judicially to advance the service, but ambitiously to get themselves a name, for having penetrated the rebels' country . . . They have produced no   5
> other effect than a ship doth in wide sea . . . While the remote parts of this land have been thus improvidently sought for and hunted after, the rebels have made war and waste in the heart of the English Pale . . . For we see by manifold experience, what madness it is for a Deputy or General to lead royal forces against naked rogues in woods   10
> and bogs, whom hounds can scarce follow, and much less men.

A criticism of the Lord Deputies' measures, 1599, in *Calendar of State Papers Ireland*, **1599–1600, pp. 362–3**

In 1601 Spanish troops landed at Kinsale in Ireland but were defeated by Lord Mountjoy, the new Lord Deputy, and by 1603 the rebels had fled and Ireland was peaceful again. However, the prolonged war with Spain and the cessation of Anglo-Spanish trade had imposed economic and social burdens on the country on an unprecedented scale. Critics of government policy were far more active than before and the monarchy was no longer immune from criticism.

Questions

1   With reference to documents **2.28** to **2.32**, explain why England was at war on so many fronts in the 1590s.
2   Explain why Elizabeth found Henry IV such a frustrating ally [**2.29–2.30**].
3   From the knowledge you already have of Spanish policy, how would you expect Philip II to react to the request made in **2.31**?

3 The Church of England and Puritanism

Elizabeth viewed the Settlement of 1559 as an act of State, designed to establish doctrine as well as to restore a proper relationship between Church and Crown. This having been achieved, in her opinion, it was no longer necessary to insist on more than outward conformity. As she said, she 'never had any meaning or intent that [her] subjects should be troubled or molested by examination or inquisition in any matter either of their faith . . . or for matters of ceremonies, as long as they shall in their outward conversation show themselves quiet and not manifestly repugnant to the laws of the realm'.

However, some of her Protestant advisers, and most of those returning from their exile under Mary, were looking for more profound changes than Elizabeth was prepared to grant. They believed they were witnessing the start of a spiritual reformation in England in which the rituals and superstition of the Roman Church would be swept away. Disagreement arose early on the subject of clerical vestments. The distinguished theologian Peter Martyr wrote to Thomas Sampson on the subject:

3.1

In the first place I exhort you, by reason of the great want of
ministers in your country, not to withdraw yourself from the function
offered you: for if you, who are as it were pillars, shall decline taking
upon yourselves the performance of ecclesiastical offices, not only will
the churches be destitute of pastors, but you will give place to wolves   5
and antichrists. By remaining without any office you will be so far
from amending those things which you dislike, that you will hardly
retain what is now conceded.

As to the square cap and external episcopal habit, I do not think
there is need of too much dispute, seeing it is unattended by   10
superstition, and in that kingdom especially there may be a political
reason for its use . . . I think, however, that if peace could obtain
between the churches of Saxony and our own with respect to

doctrine, this sort of garments would never make a separation . . .
You may therefore use those habits either in preaching, or in the   15
administration of the Lord's supper, provided however you persist in
speaking and teaching against the use of them.

**Martyr to Sampson, 1 February 1560, in *Zurich letters*, vol. 2,
pp. 38–41**

The dispute between those who accepted the established Church and those
who did not was soon to break out. In 1563 those seeking radical reform
introduced into Convocation a set of Articles removing all superstitution
and papistry:

3.2

> **2** That in all parish churches the minister in common prayer turn
> his face towards the common people; and there distinctly read the
> divine service appointed, where all the people assembled may hear
> and be edified.
>
> **3** That in ministering the sacrament of baptism, the ceremony of   5
> making the cross in the child's forehead may be omitted, as tending
> to superstition.
>
> **4** That forasmuch as divers communicants are not able to kneel
> during the time of the communion, for age, sickness and sundry other
> infirmities, and some also superstitiously both kneel and knock; that   10
> order of kneeling may be left to the discretion of the ordinary within
> his jurisdiction.
>
> **5** That it be sufficient for the minister, in time of saying divine
> service and ministering of the sacraments, to use a surplice; and that
> no minister say service or minister the sacraments but in a comely   15
> garment or habit.

Puritan Articles, 1563, in Strype, *Annals*, vol. 1, pp. 502–3

Although the move to accept these Articles was defeated – by just one vote
– it was clear that there was disorder in the Church and that the Royal
Injunctions of 1559 were not being obeyed. This was hardly surprising
when even some of the bishops, including Bishops Parkhurst of Norwich
and Grindal of London, were sympathetic to the Puritan demands. It
needed a sharp letter from the Queen to Archbishop Parker to persuade
him to enforce uniformity of rite and ceremony:

3.3

We thought, until this present, that by the regard which you, being
the primate and metropolitan would have had hereto according to
your office . . . these errors, tending to breed some schism or
deformity in the church, should have been stayed and appeased. But
perceiving very lately . . . that the same doth rather begin to increase   5
. . . we . . . have certainly determined to have all such diversities . . .
as breed nothing but contention . . . and are also against the laws,
good usages and ordinances of our realm, to be reformed and
repressed . . . And therefore, we do by these our present letters . . .
straitly charge you . . . to confer with the bishops your brethren . . .   10
and cause to be truly understood what varieties, novelties and
diversities there are in our clergy . . . either in doctrine or in
ceremonies and rites of the church, or in the manners, usages and
behaviours of the clergy themselves . . . and thereupon . . . to
proceed by order . . . of such laws and ordinances as are provided by   15
act of Parliament . . .

**Queen Elizabeth to Matthew Parker, 25 January 1565 in J. Bruce and
T. T. Perowne, (eds.), *Correspondence of Matthew Parker*, 1853, No.
CLXX**

In his efforts to carry out the Queen's wishes, Parker encountered much
opposition from the clergy in London. However, he was strengthened by
the knowledge that continental reformers such as Bucer, Martyr and
Bullinger, had declared that vestments were 'things indifferent' and not
important enough to risk schism. With his *Book of Advertisements* of 1566,
Archbishop Parker largely succeeded in enforcing conformity on the
clergy. But it was clear that the issue of wearing vestments would now be
divisive. The Queen's insistence on conformity would inevitably force the
more radical Protestants to follow their consciences and become nonconformists. The problem is illustrated in a letter written by Bullinger in
1565:

3.4

For since the great end of the ministry is the edification and
preservation of the church, we have need of great circumspection, lest
we should depart from this, even while we are defending a cause,
which in itself is good and holy. Nor are we only to consider what is

now the state of that church which we think of forsaking, but also   5
what it will be when we have left it. If it be certain that it will
improve, we are at liberty to depart; but if, on the contrary, it will
suffer loss, we are not to give place to wicked and treacherous
workmen . . . And since it is expressly provided, as you write me
word, in that proclamation, that the square caps and surplices are to   10
be retained without any superstitious conceit, I think that sufficient
consideration has, at the same time, been shown to your consciences.

Bullinger to Horn, 3 November 1565, in *Zurich Letters I*, pp. 341–4

Parker's drive to achieve conformity may have taken him further than he
originally intended: unity had been enforced within the Church but only at
the expense of even greater division within the Christian community.
Many found it impossible to conform, even though this created schism in
the Protestant ranks.

3.5

A man qualified with inward gifts for lack of outward shows is
punished, and a man outwardly conformable, inwardly clean
unfurnished, is let alone, yea exalted. The painful preacher for his
labour is beaten, the unpreaching prelate, offending in greater,
escapes scot-free. The learned man without his cap is afflicted, the   5
capped man without learning is not touched. Is not this directly to
break God's laws? Is not this Pharisee? Is not this to wash the
outside of the cup and leave the inward part uncleansed? Why do you
trust known adversaries and mistrust your brethren? We confess one
faith of Jesus Christ; we preach one doctrine, we acknowledge one   10
ruler in earth over all things. Saving of this we are of your
judgement. Shall we be used so for a surplice? Shall brethren
persecute brethren for a forked cap devised of singularity of him that
is our foreign enemy? Now shall we fight for the Popish coat, his
head and body being banished?

**Humphrey to the Ecclesiastical Commission, 1565, in Dixon, *History
of the Church of England*, 1878, vol. 6, pp. 61–63.**

Questions

1   Explain the significance of the following phrases:
      (i) 'give place to wolves and antichrists' [3.1, lines 5–6].
      (ii) 'the square cap and external episcopal habit' [3.1, line 9].

(iii) 'the churches of Saxony [**3.1, line 13**].

2   Is there anything in document **3.2** which strikes you as at variance with the Settlement described in Chapter 1?

3   Explain the significance of the phrase 'primate and metropolitan' [**3.3, line 2**].

4   Why do you suppose that Elizabeth took so harsh a line in her letter to Parker [**3.3**]?

5   Explain the significance of the following phrases:
    (i) 'without any superstitious conceit' [**3.4, line 11**].
    (ii) 'for lack of outward shows' [**3.5, line 1**].
    (iii) 'the painful preacher for his labour is beaten [**3.5, lines 3–4**].

6   Compare the arguments contained in documents **3.1** and **3.4** with those in **3.5**.

7   Is it clear why Humphrey [**3.5**] cannot accept the advice of continental Protestant leaders like Bullinger [**3.4**]?

Unlike Catholicism, which was a religion of ritual and ceremony, Protestantism was much concerned with the 'Word'. For the Puritans especially, the Church had a proselytising function. The Church needed effective preachers so that the Scriptures could be brought to the people, from the pulpit. The 1559 Injunctions had laid down a minimum standard:

3.6

All deans, archdeacons, parsons, vicars . . . shall preach in their churches one sermon every month of the year at the least, wherein they shall . . . exhort their hearers to the works of faith, as mercy and charity, especially prescribed and commanded in scripture; and that the works devised by man's fantasies, besides scripture, (as wandering   5 of pilgrimages, setting up of candles, praying upon beads, or such like superstition) have . . . great threatenings and maledictions of God, for that they be things tending to idolatry and superstition.

Also, that every parson, vicar, curate and stipendiary priest, being under the degree of a master of art, shall provide . . . within three   10 months after this visitation the New Testament both in Latin and in English, with paraphrases upon the same, conferring the one with the other. And the bishops . . . in their synods and visitations, shall examine the said ecclesiastical persons how they have profited in the study of holy scripture.   15
Also, because through lack of preachers in many places of the queen's

realms and dominions the people continue in ignorance and
blindness, all parsons, vicars and curates shall read in their churches
every Sunday one of the Homilies, which are and shall be set forth
for the same purpose by the queen's authority.

**Royal Injunctions, 1559, in A. Sparrow, *Collection of Articles,
Injunctions, Canons . . . of the Church of England*, 1661, pp. 63–80**

Naturally there was a shortage of men with the right qualifications and
bishops were forced to resort to poor quality candidates. This angered the
Puritans, who felt that without adequate preaching the people would
remain in ignorance. In fact, many church-goers seemed quite content to
remain in ignorance:

3.7

And for my parishioners, they are a kind of people that love a pot of
ale better than a pulpit, and a corn-rick better than a church door,
who, coming to divine service more for fashion than devotion, are
contented after a little capping and kneeling, coughing and spitting,
to help me to sing out a psalm, and sleep at the second lesson, or   5
awake to stand up at the gospel, and say 'Amen' at the peace of God,
and stay till the banns of matrimony be asked, or till the clerk have
cried a pied stray bullock, a black sheep or a gray mare, and then, for
that some dwell far off, be glad to be gotten home to dinner.

**Nicholas Breton, 'A merrie dialogue betwixt the take and mistaker',
1603, in A. Nicholl, *The Elizabethans*, p. 53, no. 132**

When Grindal, now Archbishop of York, began his visitation of the
province of York in 1571, one of his concerns was to discover:

3.8

. . . whether there be any innkeepers, alewives, victuallers or tipplers,
that suffer or do permit any person or persons in their houses to eat,
drink, or play at cards, tables or such like games in the time of
common prayer or sermon on the Sundays or Holy Days; and
whether there be any shops set open on Sundays or Holy days, or   5
any butchers or others, that commonly use to sell meat, or other

things in the time of common prayer, preaching, or reading of the Homilies.

Archbishop Grindal's Articles for the Province of York, 1571, in W. H. Frere, *Visitation Articles and Injunctions*, vol. 3, p. 267

Questions

1 What do you understand by the following phrases:
   (i) 'the Homilies' [**3.6, line 19, 3.8, line 8**]
   (ii) 'works devised by man's fantasies' [**3.6, line 5**].
   (iii) 'more for fashion than devotion' [**3.7, line 3**]?
2 What evidence is there that Elizabeth intended to impose a stricter religious settlement than had existed before? [**3.6 to 3.8**].
3 One historian has written that 'the Elizabethan Church had a greater problem with the many who ignored it than with the few who defied it'. How far do documents **3.1** to **3.8** demonstrate this?

In 1570 a far more radical threat to the Elizabethan Settlement was initiated by the Cambridge theologian Thomas Cartwright. He claimed that it was clear from his study of the Acts of the Apostles that the early church system of committees of elders should replace the whole ecclesiastical hierarchy of archbishops, bishops and archdeacons. Although Cartwright was dismissed and forced to flee the country, this was merely the beginning of a conflict which would lead to the development of Presbyterianism in England. Failing to achieve reform by statute in 1571, supporters of Presbyterianism concentrated on publicising their proposals in two Admonitions to the Parliament, the second of which was almost certainly written by Cartwright himself:

3.9

The outward marks whereby a true Christian church is known are preaching of the word purely, ministering the sacraments sincerely, and ecclesiastical discipline . . . Touching the first, namely the ministry of the word, although it must be confessed that the substance of doctrine by many delivered is sound and good, yet herein it faileth, that neither the ministers thereof are according to God's word proved, elected, called or ordained . . . whereas in the old church . . . no idolatrous sacrificers or heathenish priests were appointed to be preachers of the gospel: but we allow . . . popish

5

massmongers, men for all seasons, King Henry's priests, King   10
Edward's priests, Queen Mary's priests, who of a truth . . . should
for the same be utterly removed. Then they taught others, now they
must be instructed themselves, and therefore like young children they
must learn catechisms . . .
Then the ministers were preachers: now bare readers . . . In those   15
days known by voice, learning and doctrine: now they must be
discerned from other by popish and antichristian apparel, as cap,
gown and tippet etc . . .
Then nothing taught but God's word: now prince's pleasures, men's
devices, popish ceremonies and antichristian rites in public pulpits   20
defended . . .
Appoint to every congregation a learned and diligent preacher.
Remove homilies, articles, injunctions . . . Take away the lordship,
the loitering, the pomp, the idleness, and livings of bishops.

**An Admonition to the Parliament, 1572, in W. H. Frere and C. E.
Douglas (eds.),** *Puritan Manifestoes*, **1907, pp. 9–19**

The Puritans considered preaching to be the most important part of the
religious process. As preachers became established, people travelled great
distances to hear them. The sermons, often given in market towns on
market day, were known by the Pauline title of 'prophesyings', and
attracted large audiences of converts and enthusiasts. The Puritan leaders
believed that such sermons were a means of raising the standards of the
clergy and developing a feeling of community on the Swiss model.
However, to Elizabeth, these activities were potentially subversive. In
1576 she ordered Edmund Grindal, who had succeeded Parker as
Archbishop of Canterbury, to suppress prophesyings. This is how Grindal
replied:

3.10

The speeches which it hath pleased you to deliver unto me, when I
last attended on your highness, concerning abridging the number of
preachers, and the utter suppression of all learned exercises and
conferences among the ministers of the church . . . have exceedingly
dismayed and discomforted me . . . I cannot marvel enough how this   5
strange opinion should once enter into your mind, that it should be
good for the church to have few preachers . . .

. . . concerning the learned exercises and conference among the
ministers of the church: I have consulted with divers of my brethren
the bishops, by letters: who think the same as I do: a thing profitable 10
to the church, and therefore expedient to be continued . . . the said
exercises, for the interpretation and exposition of the scriptures . . .
are both profitable to increase knowledge among the ministers, and
tendeth to the edifying of the hearers . . .
Pray you to consider these two short petitions . . . 15
    The first is that you would refer all these ecclesiastical matters
which touch religion, or the doctrine and discipline of the church,
unto the bishops and divines of your realm . . . For indeed they are
things to be judged, as an ancient father writeth: in the church, or a
synod, not in a palace. 20
    The second petition . . . is this: that, when you deal in matters of
faith and religion . . . you would not use to pronounce so resolutely
and peremptorily, as from authority . . . but always remember that in
God's causes the will of God, and not the will of any earthly
creature, is to take place. It is the antichristian voice of the pope, 'So 25
I will have it; so I command; let my will stand for a reason'.
    Remember, madam, that you are a mortal creature, 'Look not only
. . . upon the purple and princely array, wherewith ye are apparalled;
but consider withal, what is that that is covered therewith. Is it not
flesh and blood? Is it not dust and ashes?'

**Grindal to Queen Elizabeth, 20 December 1576, in W. Nicholson,
(ed.), *Remains of Edmund Grindal*, 1843, pp. 376–390**

This was a courageous letter but Grindal's refusal to suppress the
prophesyings resulted in his suspension from office. The split between
Puritan views and those of the Queen was now clear.
    In a letter to the bishops in 1577, Elizabeth demanded the suppression of
the prophesyings, or 'exercises' as they were sometimes known:

3.11

Considering for the great abuse that have been in sundry places of
our realm, by reason of our aforesaid assemblies, called exercises, and
for that the same are not . . . warranted by us, or by our laws; we
will and straitly charge you, that you do charge the same forthwith to
cease . . . but if any shall attempt, or continue, or renew the same, we 5

will you not only to commit them unto prison as maintainers of
disorders, but also to advertise us, or our council, of the names and
qualities of them, and of their maintainers and abettors . . .
And in these things we charge you to be so careful and vigilant, as by
your negligence, if we should hear of any person attempting to offend   10
in the premises without your correction or information to us, we be
not forced to make some example or reformation of you according to
your deserts.

Queen Elizabeth to the bishops, 8 May 1577, in W. Nicholson (ed.),
***Remains of Edmund Grindal*, 1843, pp. 467–9**

Questions

1   What do you understand by the following:
     (i) 'men for all seasons' [**3.9, line 10**]
     (ii) 'now bare readers' [**3.9, line 15**]?
2   How are the arguments in **3.9** different from earlier criticisms of the
     Elizabethan Settlement?
3   What were the main differences between the views of the Queen and
     her Archbishop with regard to prophesyings, as revealed in **3.10** and
     3.11?
4   Does Grindal's view of the Royal Supremacy [**3.10**] differ from
     Cartwright's [**3.9**]?

However, although Elizabeth was Supreme Governor of the Church, she
found it impossible to control church affairs at parish level: congregations
often had the right to appoint clergy, and powerful local figures were able
to protect preachers.

By the 1570s those men, like Edwin Sandys, who had returned from
exile under Mary to help make the compromise Settlement of 1559, were
finding their views challenged by younger people. By agreeing to conform
and stay within the Elizabethan Church, they found that they had
sacrificed their positions as leaders of radical thought. Few had the courage
of Edmund Grindal, to challenge royal authority from within the Church.
In 1573 Sandys wrote to Bullinger, describing the state of religion in
England:

3.12

New orators are rising up from among us, foolish young men, who,
while they despise authority, and admit of no superior, are seeking
the complete overthrow and rooting up of our whole ecclesiastical
polity . . . accept this summary of the question at issue . . .

1   The civil magistrate has no authority in ecclesiastical matters. He 5
is only a member of the church . . .

2   The church of Christ admits of no other government than that by
presbyteries . . .

3   The names and authority of archbishops, archdeacons, deans,
chancellors . . . should be altogether removed from the church of 10
Christ . . .

5   The choice of ministers of necessity belongs to the people.

6   The goods, possessions, lands, revenues, titles, honours . . .
relating to bishops or cathedrals . . . should be taken away forthwith
and for ever . . . 15

There are many other things of the same kind, not less absurd, and
which I shall not mention; none of which, as far as I can judge, will
make for the advantage and peace of the church, but for her ruin and
confusion. Take away authority, and the people will rush headlong
into everything that is bad.

Edwin Sandys to Henry Bullinger, 15 August 1573, *Zurich Letters*,
No. XCIV

Elizabeth's determination to overcome divisions within the Church took
on a new intensity when John Whitgift succeeded Grindal as Archbishop of
Canterbury in 1583. Whitgift had conducted a literary campaign against
Cartwright and the Presbyterians throughout the 1570s, and he knew
that he had royal backing for his efforts to enforce the following three
articles:

3.13

That none be permitted to preach, read, catechize, minister the
sacraments, or to execute any other ecclesiastical function . . . unless
he consent and subscribe to these Articles following . . .

1   That her Majesty, under God, hath, and ought to have, the
sovereignty and rule over all manner of persons born within her 5
realms . . . either ecclesiastical or temporal, soever they be . . .

2   That the Book of Common Prayer, and of ordering bishops,
priests and deacons, containeth in it nothing contrary to the word of

God . . . and that he himself will use the form of the said book
prescribed in public prayer and administration of the sacraments, and   10
none other.

3   That he alloweth the book of Articles, agreed upon by the
archbishops and bishops of both provinces, and the whole clergy in
the Convocation holden at London in the year of our Lord God 1562
. . . and that he believeth all the Articles therein contained to be   15
agreeable to the word of God.

**Three Articles, 1583, in J. Strype, *The Life and Acts of John Whitgift*,
vol. 1, pp. 229–30**

Whitgift used the Court of High Commission to seek out non-conformist
members of the clergy and submit them to the Three Articles. Those who
could not agree in conscience to all three, were to be deprived of their
livings. The inquisitorial methods of the High Commission particularly
affected the Puritans. Burghley wrote to Whitgift about the methods being
employed:

3.14

I sent for the register, who brought me the articles, which I have
read and find so curiously penned, so full of branches and
circumstances as I think the inquisitors of Spain use not so many
questions to comprehend and trap their preys . . . in charity, I think
they ought not to answer to all these nice points, except they were   5
very notorious offenders in papistry or heresy . . . I favour no sensual
and wilful recusants. But I conclude that, according to my simple
judgement, this kind of proceeding is too much savouring of the
Romish inquisition and is rather a device to seek for offenders than to
reform any.

**Lord Burghley to Archbishop Whitgift, 1 July 1584, in J. Strype, *The
Life and Acts of John Whitgift*, vol. 3, pp. 105–6**

Burghley was able to persuade Whitgift to soften his measures on this
occasion, but concessions from the Archbishop or Elizabeth herself were
rare. Using the High Commission, Whitgift was able to break the back of
the Elizabethan Puritan movement. This short extract from a poem reflects
a contemporary view:

3.15

Who would imagine yonder sober man,
That same devout meal-mouth'd precisian,
That cries 'Good Brother', 'Kind sister', makes a duck
After the antique grace, can' always pluck
A sacred book out of his civil hose,   5
and at th'op'ning, and at stomach's close
Says with a turn'd-up eye a solemn grace
On half an hour; then with silken face
Smiles on the holy crew, and then doth cry,
'O manners! O times of impurity!'   10
Who thinks that this good man
Is a vile, sober, damned politician?
Not I, till with his bait of purity
He bit me sore in deepest usury.
No Jew, no Turk, would use a Christian   15
so inhumanely as this Puritan.

W. K., 'The Metamorphosis of Pygmalion's Image', quoted in G. B.
Harrison, *A Second Elizabethan Journal*, p. 280

Questions

1   What do you understand by the following phrases:
      (i) 'so full of branches and circumstances' [3.14, lines 2–3]
      (ii) 'too much savouring of the Romish in question' [3.14, lines 8–9]
      (iii) 'He bit me sore in deepest usury' [3.15, line 14]
2   To what extent do you feel that Sandys represents the government
    line on religious thinking [3.12]? How does this compare with his
    earlier views [1.14]?
3   What were the Puritans' main objections to Whitgift's Three Articles
    [3.13]?
4   How effective do you feel that men like Leicester and Burghley were
    in moderating Elizabeth's religious policies?
5   How accurate a view of Elizabethan Puritanism is contained in the
    contemporary poem [3.15]?

Small groups of Radicals, despairing of any hope that the national Church
could be adequately reformed, 'separated' themselves from it and set up
independent churches at various times in the 1590s. Under men like

Browne, Barrow and Greenwood, such congregations proved a great thorn in the side of the flesh of the authorities, to the extent that their leaders were seized and executed for sedition in 1593.

3.16

9th March   Many of the sect called Barrowists have been taken at one of their meetings at Islington. One, Daniel Buck, a scrivener, was today examined before Justice Young. Concerning the bishops he thinks that they have no spiritual authority over the rest of the Church. Being demanded who was their pastor, he said one Mr   5
Francis Johnson; and about six months since this Johnson delivered the sacrament of baptism to seven persons; but they had neither godfathers nor godmothers. He took water and washed the faces of them that were baptised, saying only in the administration of the sacrament, 'I do baptise thee in the name of the Father, of the Son,   10
and of the Holy Ghost', without using any other ceremony therein, as is usually observed according to the Book of Common Prayer.

6th April   Barrow and Greenwood, that were respited last week, were hanged early this morning. It is said that the execution proceeded through the malice of the bishops towards the Lower   15
House because of the dislike shown yesterday to the Bishop's Bill against the Puritans. The reprieve was through a supplication to the Lord Treasurer that in a land where no papist was ever put to death for religion theirs should not be the first blood shed who concurred about faith with what was professed in the country and desired   20
conference to be convinced of their errors.

G. B. Harrison, *An Elizabethan Journal*, pp. 214 and 222

The remnants of the Barrowists moved to Amsterdam. Meanwhile, the Elizabethan Church continued as an uneasy alliance. People like Whitgift and Bancroft had been unable to counter Cartwright's argument that the Scriptures, being the revealed word of God, were better guides to organising the church than the opinions of men. However, Richard Hooker, in his great work, *Of the Laws of Ecclesiastical Polity*, was able to point out that 'In those things whereof the Scriptures appointest no certainty, the use of the people of God or the ordinance of the fathers must serve for a law'.

Hooker failed in his attempt to unite the Elizabethan Church. Far from it, his appeal to tradition and the rule of the Church Fathers appealed more to Catholics than to the Calvinists. The end of Elizabeth's reign saw the Puritans weaker in the House of Commons, yet stronger among the general population, which was not easily swayed by philosophical discussion. With the death of Elizabeth and the accession of James VI, from Calvinist Scotland, the Puritans might hope for a better future.

4 Catholicism under Elizabeth

The religion of England had changed three times in as many reigns and, in 1559, there were many who felt that it might change again. Debate over the royal succession added to the general climate of uncertainty. Away from the centre of affairs at Westminster, people frequently clung to traditional forms of worship, to what they called the 'old religion'.

In the early part of Elizabeth's reign rumours of religious changes were common, and as a result many of the clergy were reluctant to dismantle altars and rood lofts, to deface images, or destroy the equipment for Mass. Many of the clergy remained Catholic in sentiment and Elizabeth's new bishops faced the difficult task of stamping out Catholic practices and enforcing conformity. The survival of Catholicism was not only confined to the more inaccessible areas of the North, as this report from Sussex showed:

4.1

In the Church of Arundel, certain altars do stand yet still to the offence of the godly, which murmur and speak much against the same . . . They have yet in the diocese, in many places, images hidden up and other popish ornaments, ready to set up the mass again within twenty four hours' warning; as in the town of Battle and 5 in the parish of Lindfield, where they be yet very blind and superstitious . . . In the town of Battle, when a preacher does come and speak against the Pope's doctrine, they will not abide but get them out of the church . . . The schoolmaster is the cause of their going out, who afterwards in corners among the people does gainsay 10 [=contradict] the preachers. It is the most popish town in all Sussex.

In some places, because the rood¹ was taken away, they painted there in that place a cross with chalk, and because that was washed away with painting, and the number of crosses standing at graves in the churchyard taken also away, they have since made crosses upon 15 the church walls within and without, and upon the pulpit and communion table in despite of the preacher . . . Many bring to church the old popish Latin primers², and use to pray upon them all

the time when the lessons are being read and in the time of the
litany. In some places the rood lofts[3] still stand, and those taken   20
down still lie in the churches ready to be put up again.

[1] 'rood' = large crucifix at the junction between the nave (where the people
     sat) and the chancel (where the clergy officiated)
[2] 'Latin primers' = layperson's prayerbooks
[3] 'rood lofts' = galleries over a screen surmounted by a large crucifix

**Report from Bishop Barlow of Chichester, 1569, in *Victoria History
of the Counties of England: Sussex*, p. 25**

However, the majority of Elizabeth's subjects obediently attended church
services on Sundays, if only to avoid the shilling fine for non-attendance.
The problem of recusancy applied more to the Catholic gentry, who were
able to afford the fine. As a result, the government adopted a cautious
approach to recusants in the early years of the reign, particularly so where
Catholic gentlemen played an important part in local government. The
bishops, however, faced a continual struggle to combat papistry amongst
the ordinary members of their dioceses, as well as to overcome the
influence of Catholics in prominent positions. This report from the Bishop
of Hereford refers to the situation in Hereford in 1564:

4.2

There be also in this diocese and county of Hereford divers fostered
and maintained that be judged and esteemed, some of them, to be
learned, which in Queen Mary's days had livings and offices in the
Church, which be mortal and deadly enemies to this religion . . .
These go from one gentleman's house to another, where they know to   5
be welcome.

**Bishop John Scory of Hereford to the Privy Council, October 1564, in
Camden Miscellany, Royal Historical Society, vol. 9, no. 8**

Catholicism remained strongest, predictably, in those areas most distant
from or most inaccessible to central government. In the North and West in
particular, the 'Old Religion' continued as it always had done, less
concerned with doctrinal issues than with the fundamentals that gave
structure to the lives of country people: like the changing seasons, births,
marriages and deaths. The new doctrines of Protestantism found it difficult
to break down the habits of centuries. Something of this traditional
attitude is seen in the following extract, in which a Catholic lady explains
her recusancy, as recorded by a contemporary biographer in the service of
the Dormer family:

4.3

I was born in such a time when holy mass was in great reverence,
and brought up in the same faith. In King Edward's time this
reverence was neglected and reproved by such as governed. In Queen
Mary's time, it was restored with much applause; and now in this
time it pleaseth the state to question them, as now they would do me,   5
who continue in this Catholic profession. The state would have these
several changes, which I have seen with mine eyes, good and
laudable. Whether it can be so, I refer it to your Lordship's
consideration. I hold me still to that wherein I was born and bred;
and find nothing taught in it but great virtue and sanctity; and so by   10
the grace of God I will live and die in it.

**Catholic lady, c. 1581, in H. Clifford, *Life of Jane Dormer, Duchess
of Feria*, 1643, pp. 38–9**

In remote areas, recusant priests often became domestic chaplains to the
gentry. Within their houses the old religious cycles of fasting and feasting,
the celebration of Easter and Christmas, marriages and christenings was
able to continue. In some ways the house became a kind of religious
community in which children, servants and tenants alike attended
services. Bishop Scory of Hereford describes such a situation:

4.4

And of these there be certain thought to have masses in their houses,
which come very seldom or not at all to church, which never received
communion since the Queen's Majesty's reign openly in the church,
which keep as it were schools in their houses of popery, deriding and
mocking this religion and the ministers thereof, which be a   5
marvellous [= remarkable] stumbling block to the Queen's Majesty's
loving subjects in this county . . . I must needs confess that I am not
able to reform these, except I should be mightily backed by your
honourable authority, and have those worshipful justices which are
deemed favourers of religion to be more earnestly aiding than they   10
have been.

**Bishop John Scory of Hereford to the Privy Council, October 1564, in
Camden Miscellany, Royal Historical Society, vol. 9, no. 8**

Questions

1   What do you understand by the following:
     (i) 'divers fostered and maintained' [**4.2, lines 1–2**]
     (ii) 'schools in their houses of popery' [**4.4, line 4**]?
2   How do documents **4.1** to **4.4** help you to understand:
     (i) the nature of English Catholicism?
     (ii) the extent of English Catholicism?
3   Is it clear from documents **4.1** to **4.4** which groups in society were
     most resistant to religious change?
4   Do these documents help you to understand why it proved
     impossible to stamp out Catholicism? What were the main handicaps
     which the bishops appear to have suffered from?

For Elizabeth the problem of her Catholic subjects could not be divorced
from her relations with the great Catholic powers on the continent: France
and Spain. In fact the persecution of Catholic recusants can be seen to
coincide with periods of crisis in international affairs. This is clearly
reflected in the Revolt of the Earls of 1569:

4.5

Proclamation by Thomas Earl of Northumberland and Charles Earl
of Westmoreland, the Queen's true and faithful subjects, to all the
same of the old and Catholic faith.
    Know ye, that we, with many other well-disposed of the nobility
and others, have promised our faith for the furtherance of this our   5
good meaning. As divers ill-disposed persons about Her Majesty
have, by their crafty dealing, otherthrown in this realm the true and
Catholic religion towards God, abused the Queen, dishonoured the
realm, and now seek to procure the destruction of this nobility, we
have gathered ourselves together to resist force by force, and rather,   10
by the help of God and you good people, to redress those things
amiss, with the restoring of all ancient customs and liberties to God
and this noble realm. If we shall not do it ourselves, we might be
reformed by strangers, to the great hazarding of the state of this our
country.

Enclosure in Earl of Sussex to the Privy Council, 17 November 1569
in *State Papers Domestic Addenda*, 1566–79, p. 110

Initially it looked as though the whole of the Far North might support the Earls. Elizabeth did not even feel confident in the loyalty of her Lord President of the North, the Earl of Sussex. Despite the Queen's misgivings, however, his loyalty was clearly to be shown in the months of crisis:

4.6

> These two Earls have, I think, been induced by evil counsel to enter into dealing with matters . . . deeper and more wicked . . . than they discovered in the beginning . . . and so by fear drawn on . . . to what was intended by those wicked counsellors at the beginning and is now . . . published; I mean the cause of religion . . .   5
> The Earls having now disobeyed your command, must either prepare force to fight, or seek to fly. If they prepare to fight, they will make religion their ground, and what force they may have in that cause I know not, nor how many will go with me against that cause . . . If they be not able to get a force, and so flee into foreign realms   10
> and make religion their ground, it is good to consider what likelihood there is of assistance there, and what peril there may be upon their return with foreign force . . .

> **Earl of Sussex to Queen Elizabeth, 15 November 1569, in *Calendar of State Papers Domestic Addenda*, 1566–79, vol. 15 pp. 107–8**

Sussex could not risk his troops in open confrontation with the rebels, as Sir Ralph Sadler explained to Cecil:

4.7

> There are not ten gentlemen in all this country that favour her proceedings in the cause of religion. The common people are ignorant, superstitious, and altogether blinded with the old popish doctrine, and therefore so favour the cause which the rebels make the colour of their rebellion, that, though their persons be here with us,   5
> their hearts are with them. And no doubt all this country had wholly rebelled if, at the beginning, my Lord Lieutenant had not wisely and stoutly handled the matter. If we should go to the field with this northern force only, they would fight faintly; for if the father be on their side, the son is on the other . . .

> **Sir Ralph Sadler to Sir William Cecil, 6 December 1569, in *Calendar of State Papers Domestic Addenda*, 1566–79, vol. 15, p. 77**

After the collapse of the rebellion, the Earl of Northumberland fled to Scotland, but was eventually handed back by the Scots. In this extract he answers questions from Lord Hunsdon:

4.8

When did you first enter into this conspiracy?

[Answer] We first began to talk of these matters when the Duke went in displeasure from Court to his house in London, and it was bruited in Yorkshire that the Council was wonderfully divided about the succession, that the Duke and other noblemen had retired to their 5 houses, and that the realm would be in a hurly-burly; so I sent to the Duke and assembled my friends, to know their inclinations. I and many gentlemen intended to join the Duke, if the quarrel were for reformation of religion or naming a successor, but not to hazard myself for the marriage . . . 10

What was the intent and meaning of the rebellion?

[Answer] Our first object in assembling was the reformation of religion and preservation of the person of the Queen of Scots, as next heir, failing issue of Her Majesty.

Examination of the Earl of Northumberland, 1572, in *Calendar of State Papers Domestic Addenda*, **1566–79, vol. 21, p. 56**

Until 1569 Elizabeth treated her Catholic subjects with considerable leniency hoping that Catholicism would gradually die out as the generation which had grown up in that faith themselves died out. What she needed was time, and her friendly relations with Spain in the 1560s were designed to give her this. However, the revolt of 1569, closely followed by the Papal Bull in 1570, forced her to react strongly to the growing threat of Catholicism, both from without and within. The Papal Bull was a disastrous miscalculation which severely harmed the position of Catholics in England:

4.9

But the number of the ungodly hath gotten such power that there is now no place in the whole world left which they have not essayed to corrupt with their most wicked doctrines; and amongst others,

Elizabeth, the pretended Queen of England, the servant of
wickedness, lendeth thereunto her helping hand, with whom, as in a   5
sanctuary, the most pernicious persons have found a refuge. This
very woman, having seized on the kingdom and monstrously usurped
the place of Supreme Head of the Church in all England . . . hath
again reduced the said kingdom into a miserable and ruinous
condition, which was so lately reclaimed to the Catholic faith and a   10
thriving condition . . .
. . . do out of the fullness of Our Apostolic power declare the
aforesaid Elizabeth as being an heretic and a favourer of heretics, and
her adherents in the matters aforesaid, to have incurred the sentence
of excommunication, and to be cut off from the unity of the Body of   15
Christ. And moreover We do declare her to be deprived of her
pretended title to the kingdom aforesaid . . . and also the nobility,
subjects and people of the said kingdom . . . to be for ever absolved
from . . . all manner of duty of dominion, allegiance, and obedience.

**Papal Bull, 'Regnans in Excelsis', 1570, in W. Camden, *History of the
Most Renowned and Victorious Princess, late Queen of England*, 1625**

Questions

1   Is the Pope's view of Elizabeth [**4.9**] effectively the same as that of
     the Northern earls [**4.5** and **4.8**]?
2   Why do you suppose the worst fears of Sir Ralph Sadler [**4.7**] were
     not realised?
3   Explain the meaning of 'to be cut off from the unity of the Body of
     Christ' [**4.9, lines 15–16**]. What were its consequences?
4   Comment on the interconnection of religion and politics in
     documents **4.5** to **4.9**.

The political crisis of 1569–70 coincided with the beginning of a Catholic
missionary effort, which produced its own pressures on Elizabeth to meet a
new challenge. Traditional English Catholicism is best exemplified by the
work of the Oxford scholars who left England on Elizabeth's accession and
went to Louvain. Their views underwent no radical change until they
were joined by a younger generation of clerks whose Catholicism was
inspired by the needs of the time and who wanted to fight heresy and win
back those who had fallen under its spell. They were unafraid to meet
danger and prepared, if necessary, to sacrifice their lives for their beliefs.
One such man was the Jesuit Edmund Campion, who wrote the following
in 1580:

4.10

1   I confess that I am, although unworthy, a priest of the Catholic Church, and through the great mercy of God vowed now these eight years into the religion of the Society of Jesus . . .

3   My charge is, of free cost, to preach the gospel, to minister the sacraments, to instruct the simple, to reform sinners, to confute   5
errors . . .

4   I never had mind [= wished] and am strictly forbidden by our father that sent me, to deal in any respect with matter of state or policy of this realm, as things which appertain not to my vocation . . .

6   I would be loth to speak anything that might sound of any   10
insolent brag or challenge, especially being now as a dead man to this world, and willing to put my head under every man's foot . . . Yet have I such a courage in avowing the majesty of Jesus my king, and such affiance [= trust] in his gracious favour, and such assurance in my quarrel, and my evidence so impregnable, and because I know   15
perfectly that no one Protestant, nor all the Protestants living . . . can maintain their doctrine in disputation, I am to sue most humbly and instantly for the combat with all and every of them . . .

8   Moreover, I doubt not but you, her Highness's Council . . . will see upon what substantial grounds our Catholic faith is built, how   20
feeble that side is which by sway of the time prevails against us, and so . . . will discountenance error when it is betrayed, and harken to those who would spend the best blood in their bodies for your salvation. Many innocent hands are lifted up to heaven for you daily by those English students whose posterity shall never die, which   25
beyond seas gathering virtue and sufficient knowledge for the purpose, are determined never to give you over, but either to win you heaven or to die upon your pikes.

Edmund Campion, 'Brag', in J. H. Pollen, *The Month*, January 1910

Deteriorating relations between England and Spain, particularly over the Netherlands, and the onset of the Jesuit mission in England, led to the issue of strict penal laws, by which Catholics could be executed as traitors. Lord Burghley published the government's view that those executed died not for their beliefs, but because they refused allegiance to Elizabeth:

4.11

And though there are many subjects known in the realm that differ in
some opinions of religion from the Church of England and that do
also not forbear to profess the same, yet in that they do also profess
loyalty and obedience to Her Majesty and offer readily in Her
Majesty's defence to impugn and resist any foreign force, though it   5
should come or be procured from the Pope himself, none of these
sort are for their contrary opinions in religion prosecuted or charged
with any crimes or pains of treason, nor yet willingly searched in
their consciences for their contrary opinions that savour not of
treason.

Burghley, *The Execution of Justice in England*, ed. R. M. Kingdom,
Folger Shakespeare Library, pp. 9–10

As the danger of a Spanish attack increased, it became particularly difficult
for the Jesuit missionaries and seminary priests, who came to England from
Douai, Rheims and Rome, to escape arrest. A whole underground system
of 'safe' houses developed and yet detection was never far away. Many
Catholic priests were arrested, tried and executed, like James Bell:

4.12

When he had thus truly fed the poor flock of Christ by word and
example, for the space of two years and more, in the month of
January anno 1584, as he was travelling alone and on foot from one
Catholic's house to another, he met with one of the common
promoters [= informers] or spies. Of whom Mr Bell (thinking him to   5
be an honest man) asked the way to a certain town. This naughty
fellow, suspecting forthwith that this good old man was a priest,
began to examine him whence he came and whither he would go. Mr
Bell making a stay [= hesitating] to answer these questions, the fellow
asked him what he was, to whom he answered boldly and freely that   10
he was a priest . . . The promoter brought the old father to a Justice
of Peace, before whom he confessed again that he was a priest, but
that he had not lived for many years together according to his priestly
function and calling, and that now he was reconciled and was
desirous to say Mass, if he knew where to have a place and other   15
things necessary for that purpose. He told the Justice also that very

lately he had received authority to hear confessions and to absolve, and that the same authority came from the Pope. . . And so was sent to Manchester and there imprisoned, sometimes in the loathsome dungeon . . . Upon Wednesday in the Assize week, this virtuous   20 father was indicted [= accused] and arraigned[1] for affirming the Pope of Rome . . . Then the judge asked him whether the Queen were supreme governor in all causes in England, as well ecclesiastical as temporal. 'No', says he, 'for she has not to judge in spiritual causes and matters of faith, but the Pope is to deal in those matters, and   25 under him bishops and priests.' 'Whose part would you take, if the Pope or any other by his authority should make wars against the Queen? 'We ought,' says he, 'to take part with the Church of God, for the Catholic religion.' . . . When he was taken off the hurdle[2], they caused him to look upon his companion that was a-quartering.   30 When he saw the hangman pull out his bowels 'O why,' says he, 'do I tarry [= delay] so long behind my sweet brother; let me make haste after him. This is a most happy day.' This being spoken, he fell to his devotions.

[1] 'arraigned' = brought before a court
[2] 'hurdle' = wooden vehicle on which traitors are drawn to their execution

'The Martyrdom of James Bell', April 1584, in *Unpublished Documents relating to the English Martyrs*, ed. J. H. Pollen, in Catholic Record Society, 1908, vol. 5, pp. 75–8

Questions

1   What do you understand by the following phrases:
     (i) 'now as a dead man to this world' [4.10, lines 11–12]
     (ii) 'by sway of the time prevails' [4.10, line 21]?
2   Campion denies any intention of interfering with the politics of England [4.10]. From the evidence in documents 4.10 to 4.12, was this a viable position for Catholic missionaries to uphold?
3   What were the main problems faced by the Catholic missionaries in England?

With the international situation moving towards open war between England and Spain, and the discovery of various plots associated with Mary Stuart inflaming passions at home, it was only a matter of time before it was declared treason simply to be a Jesuit or seminary priest. This was confirmed in an Act of Parliament in 1585 and Jesuits and Catholic Priests were ordered to be driven from the realm.

As rumours of Spanish preparation of an Armada reached England the Council turned to action against the enemy within:

4.13

> Amongst other things, considering how, of late years, divers of her
> subjects by the means of bad instruments have been withdrawn from
> the due obedience they owe to her Majesty and her laws, insomuch as
> divers of them most obstinately have refused to come to church, to
> prayers and divine service . . . it is hardly adventured to repose that   5
> trust in them which is to be looked for in her other good subjects;
> and it is also certain that such as should mean to invade the realm
> would never attempt the same, but upon hope (which the fugitives
> and rebels abroad do give and assure them) of those bad members
> that already are known to be recusants. It is therefore thought meet   10
> in these doubtful times, they should be looked to [= investigated] and
> restrained, as they shall neither be able to give assistance to the
> enemy, nor that the enemy should have any hope of relief and
> succour by them. Wherefore her Majesty's pleasure is, your lordship
> shall cause due enquiry to be made what number of recusants are in   15
> that county, and what quality and ability they be of . . . and
> thereupon to cause the most obstinate and noted persons to be
> committed to such prisons as are fittest for their safekeeping. The
> rest that are of value, and not so obstinate, to be referred to the
> custody of some ecclesiastical persons and other gentlemen well   20
> affected.

> **Privy Council to Lieutenants of Sussex, 4 January 1588, in *Acts of the
> Privy Council*, 1587–8, pp. 35–9**

With the advent of the Armada in 1588 Catholics were faced with an unavoidable choice. Membership of the Church of Rome meant obedience to the Pope, who had declared war on England and was acting through Spain to overthrow Elizabeth. Burghley's equation of active papistry and treason was now accepted by most English people. Elizabeth herself had never been keen to persecute Catholics for their religious beliefs, but if they proved to be a threat to the safety of her realm she would be relentless.

The battle lines were drawn up in 1588, when Cardinal William Allen issued his 'Admonition to the Nobility and People of England':

4.14

Briefly and plainly we will set down what manner of woman she is
against whom this holy enterprise is made . . .
She usurped by Luciferian pride the title of Supreme Ecclesliastical
Governor, a thing in a woman, in all men's memory, unheard of nor
tolerable to the masters of her own sect, and to Catholics in the world   5
most ridiculous, absurd and detestable . . .
She unlawfully intruded herself . . . into possession of the crown of
England . . . being indeed taken and known for an incestuous
bastard, begotten and born in sin, of an infamous courtesan Anne
Boleyn. She did immediately on her said intrusion, violently against   10
all law and order, to the perdition of infinite souls, abolish the whole
Catholic religion and faith . . .
She did at the same time abolish or profane all the holy sacraments of
Christ's Church . . .
She hath employed the riches of the realm to set up and sustain   15
rebels and heretics against their natural princes, to the great dishonor
of our nation . . . A public piracy and robbery both by sea and land
has been authorized by her letters of marque, and she has otherwise
permitted divers wicked persons to despoil whom they like, making
certain that some piece of the gain returns to some of her own chief   20
councillors and officers.
      In which sort . . . she has exalted one special extortioner . . . to
serve her filthy lust, whereof to have the more freedom and interest,
he . . . caused his own wife cruelly to be murdered . . . he is
advanced to high office, degree and excessive wealth, and is become   25
her chief leader in all her wicked and unwonted course.

**Cardinal William Allen, 'Admonition to the Nobility and People of
England', 1588, pp. 8–29**

Questions

1   How convincing are the arguments in document **4.13** for the
      internment of Catholics?
2   What do you understand by the following phrases in document **4.14**:
      (i) 'Luciferian pride' **[line 3]**
      (ii) 'incestuous bastard' **[lines 8–9]**

(iii) 'the perdition of infinite souls' [line 11]
(iv) 'letters of marque' [line 18]?
3   Who do you think Elizabeth's 'special extortioner' was [4.14, line 22]?
4   What techniques does the polemic writer use to gain effect and what dangers are there for the historian using such evidence [4.14]?

William Allen's pamphlet had been intended for circulation after the Spanish invasion began. However, with the failure of the Armada it was an embarrassment to most Catholics who had remained loyal to Elizabeth. They resented the way that men like Allen and Parsons had identified Catholicism with the Spanish attempt to conquer England. The argument used by the Catholic missionaries, that their purpose was purely spiritual, seemed to be undermined by the obviously political nature of Allen's manifesto.

At the end of Elizabeth's reign the Catholic threat seemed less dangerous. The efforts of missionary priests had won converts but the stronghold of the faith was still the Catholic gentry, who had remained loyal to the Queen and yet had not compromised their belief in the 'old religion'. This report shows the state of religion in some Northern areas in the 1590s:

4.15

> Report to the Council on the condition of Lancashire and Cheshire.
> Small reformation has been made there by the Ecclesiastical
> Commission, as may appear by the emptiness of churches on Sundays
> and holidays, and the multitudes of bastards and drunkards . . . The
> youth for the most part are trained up by such as profess papistry; no   5
> examination is had of schools and schoolmasters. The proclamation
> for the apprehension of seminarists, Jesuits and mass priests, and for
> calling home children from parts beyond sea is not executed, nor are
> their Lordships' letters commanding the justices to call before them
> quarterly all parsons, vicars, curates, churchwardens, and sworn men,   10
> and examine them on how the statutes of 1 and 23 Eliz. as to
> resorting to churches are obeyed . . . Some of the coroners and
> justices, and their families, do not frequent church, and many of
> them have not communicated at the Lord's supper since the
> beginning of Her Majesty's reign. The seminaries in many places   15
> have lately offered disputations against the settled religion; but
> nothing has been said to them . . .

The recusants have spies about the Commissioners, to give intelligence when anything is intended against them, and some of the bailiffs attending upon the Commissioners are entertained for that 20 purpose, so that the recusants may shift out of the way and avoid being apprehended; some example ought to be made of the bailiffs, as a terror to others.

Report on the State of the North, 1591, in *Calendar of State Papers Domestic*, **1591–4, pp. 158–9**

Questions

1 Does document **4.15** constitute evidence that the authorities were losing the battle for uniformity of religion by 1603?
2 Why might Catholicism have remained stronger in this region than in others?
3 What was the state of religion in 1603?

5 Elizabeth and the local communities

In 1558 England was not a united country. Apart from the obvious religious divisions, there were other more subtle ways in which local differences asserted themselves in politics. In times of national crisis, as in 1588, a charismatic leader like Elizabeth could appeal to a spirit of patriotism, but this was far from common. The counties reflected vastly different local experiences, not merely in terms of geography or economic patterns. In some cases one or two powerful families dominated the economic, social and political life of an area, while in others a group of higher gentry would vie with each other for dominance. Northern areas were less well developed than those of the South and were under-represented both at Court and on the Queen's Council.

Under the Tudors major changes took place in the system of local administration. By 1585 every shire in England was under the authority of a Lord Lieutenant, who was usually a nobleman and often member of the Privy Council too. Their responsibility was to maintain security and administer the government's military policies at local level. In 1586 Sir Christopher Hatton was appointed Lord Lieutenant for Northamptonshire:

5.1

> To our trusty and well-beloved counsellor Sir Christopher Hatton knight, our Vicechamberlain, greeting. Know you that for the great and singular trust and confidence we have in your approved fidelity, wisdom and circumspection [= prudence], we have assigned . . . you to be our lieutenant within our county of Northampton . . . And do   5
> by these presents give full power and authority unto you that you from time to time may levy, gather and call together all and singular our subjects . . . dwelling . . . within our said county . . . And them to try, array [= assemble] and put in readiness, and them also . . . to cause to be armed and weaponed, and to take the musters[1] of them   10
> from time to time in places meet for that purpose . . . And also . . . men of arms as other horsemen, archers and footmen, of all kinds and

degrees meet and apt for the wars, to conduct and lead as well against
all and singular our enemies, as also against all and singular rebels,
traitors and other offenders . . . And to do . . . all and singular other   15
things which shall be requisite for the levying and government of our
said subjects for the conservation of our person and peace . . . and
use against the said enemies . . . the law called the martial law . . .
and of such offenders apprehended . . . to save whom you shall think
good to be saved and to slay . . . such . . . of them as you shall think   20
meet . . . And further we give you full power and authority, for the
execution of this our commission, to appoint and assign in our said
county . . . muster-masters and one provost-marshal[2]. Which provost-
marshal shall execute and use the martial law in case of any invasion or
rebellion in conducting any numbers of men of war against the said   25
invaders, traitors or rebels . . . And for so much as it may be that
there shall be just cause as now there is for you to be attendant upon
our person, or to be otherwise employed in our service, whereby this
our service of lieutenancy committed to your fidelity cannot be by
you executed . . . therefore we give unto you authority to appoint . . .   30
our trusty and well-beloved Sir John Spencer knight, Sir Richard
Knightley knight, and Sir Edward Montague knight to be your
deputies.

[1] 'musters' = gatherings of troops
[2] 'muster-masters and one provost-marshal' = officers in charge of local
   military forces

**Queen Elizabeth's Commission to Sir Christopher Hatton, 12
September 1586, in J. Wake (ed.), *Musters, Beacons and Subsidies in
the County of Northampton*, pp. 1–4**

The latter half of Elizabeth's reign was dominated by war and by rumours
of war. After 1585, England was fighting at sea, in Ireland and on the
continent, and facing the very real threat of Spanish invasion, but the
military system was quite inadequate to cope with these wide-ranging
demands. In 1573, the Privy Council had ordered that select groups from
the county levies should be given special training. These groups were
known as Trained Bands. In theory the Queen was to have:

5.2

. . . perfect knowledge of the numbers, qualities, abilities and
sufficiencies of all of her subjects from the age of 16 years upward

that may be found able to bear armour or to use weapon on
horseback or foot; and out of that total and universal number being
viewed, mustered and registered, to have a convenient and sufficient   5
number of the most able to be chosen and collected to be by the
reasonable charge of the inhabitants in every shire tried, armed and
weaponed, and so consequently taught and trained for to use, handle
and exercise their horses, armour, shot and other weapons both on
horseback and on foot for the service and defence of her Majesty, her   10
crown and realm, against all attempts, both inward and outward.

**Harleian MSS 6844, f. 16, in C. G. Cruikshank, *Elizabeth's Army*,
p. 24**

However, in practice there was to be constant trouble between local and
central government over the costs incurred by these military reforms.
Between 1585 and 1603, over 100,000 men had to be levied for service
overseas. By law these men could not be taken from the Trained Bands,
whose task was to serve in England only. Pressed soldiers needed weapons,
uniforms and training, problems which came within the sphere of the Lord
Lieutenant and his deputies.

After soldiers had been raised in an area, they needed to be moved to join
the army. 'Coat and conduct' money was supposed to be raised locally and
later repaid by the Exchequer, but repayment was a very slow process.
Furthermore, local communities were responsible for the local arsenal,
which had to be kept equipped with weapons in case of invasion or other
emergencies. Coastal counties were held responsible for building and
repairing coastal forts and beacons.

The issue of Muster-masters was particularly controversial during
Elizabeth's reign. These ex-professional soldiers were appointed by central
government to assist with the training of local levies and their officers.
However, local authorities resented having to pay their salaries and where
possible they dispensed with their services. As a result the counties often
filled the ranks for overseas service with vagabonds and criminals.
Barnaby Rich writes of this practice:

5.3

Our manner of appointing of soldiers, is yet more confused than the
rest, they be appointed in the country as it pleaseth Master
Constable: for if there be any within his circuit, that he is in
displeasure withall, he thinks it some part of revenge, if he sets him
forth to be a soldier, but if Master Constable be in love and charity   5

with his neighbours, then some odd fellow must be picked out that doth least good in the parish, it is no matter for his conditions, they think he cannot be too ill to make a soldier of. In London when they set forth soldiers, either they scour their prisons of thieves, or their streets of rogues and vagabonds, for he that is bound to find a man, will seek such a one as were better lost than found.

Barnaby Rich, 'Alarm to England', fol. K3

Shakespeare's Falstaff takes up the story:

5.4

I have misused the king's press damnably. I have got, in exchange of a hundred and fifty soldiers, three hundred and odd pounds. I press me none but good householders, yeomen's sons; inquire me out contracted bachelors, such as had been twice on the banns; such a commodity of warm slaves, as had as lieve hear the devil as a drum, such as fear the report of a caliver . . . and they have bought out their services; and now my whole charge consists of ancients, corporals, lieutenants, gentlemen of companies – slaves as ragged as Lazarus in the painted cloth, where the glutton's dogs licked his sores; and such as indeed were never soldiers, but discarded unjust serving-men, younger sons to younger brothers, revolted tapsters, and ostlers trade-fall'n; the cankers of a calm world and a long peace; ten times more dishonourable ragged than any old-fazed ancient; and such have I to fill up the rooms of them as have bought out their services that you would think that I had a hundred and fifty tattered prodigals lately come from swine-keeping, from eating draff and husks. A mad fellow met me on the way, and told me I had unloaded all the gibbets and pressed the dead bodies.

W. Shakespeare, *Henry IV*, Part 1, Act IV, Scene 2

Questions

1 Explain the following:
   (i) 'martial law' [5.1, line 18]
   (ii) 'the king's press' [5.4, line 1]
   (iii) 'contracted bachelors' [5.4, line 4]
2 Summarise the powers of Lords Lieutenant [5.1].

3   What do documents **5.1** to **5.4** suggest were the main weaknesses of
       the muster system?
4   Why, despite these weaknesses, do you think that Elizabethan
       ministers came up with no better systems?

The marked reluctance of shires to contribute to the needs of war can also
be seen in the raising of 'Ship Money'. It had long been the prerogative of
the Crown to commandeer ships in time of war, or to accept money instead
of ships. Towards the end of Elizabeth's reign the burden fell heavily on
coastal ports, as well as on London, and the levy of Ship Money was
extended to inland counties as well. As a result Elizabeth encountered
strong local opposition:

5.5

(a)   An open letter to Sir John Savile knight, and the rest of the
Justices of the Peace in the West Riding of the county of York.
Though all other the maritime counties of the realm have contributed
with the port towns in like charge, yet you having been so often and
earnestly required have shown yourselves to be led rather with a   5
popular affection of some that affect to bear a sway [= influence] or
rule amongst you, and have not only refused to show your duties in
contributing to so necessary and honourable a service, but have
eluded our earnest direction by dilatory, frivolous and framed
[= false] excuses, some of you having proceeded so far to call in   10
question by what authority in those public actions that concern the
defence of the realm such contributions be demanded.

(b)   A letter directed to the Lord Mayor of the city of London.
Whereas her Majesty has of late had occasion to make great levies of
men and to burden that city with other extraordinary charges . . .   15
nevertheless, her Majesty being given to understand that upon these
and other like occasions the exempt places within the city of London
do not only refuse to furnish soldiers for their parts, and to
contribute ratably as they ought to do, but do retain such persons as
absent themselves and have recourse thither, thereby seeking to avoid   20
the impressing[1], to the hindrance and defrauding of her Majesty's
service . . . For redress of this abuse . . . we should direct your
lordship . . . to require the chief officers of all the exempt and

privileged places . . . shall furnish and supply those numbers which upon conference between you and them shall be thought convenient.

¹ 'impressing' = conscription of troops

Acts of the Privy Council, 1598

Questions

1   Explain the following:
    (i) 'led rather with a popular affection' [5.5(a), lines 5–6]
    (ii) 'extraordinary charges' [5.5(b), line 15]
    (iii) 'exempt and privileged places' [5.5(b), lines 23–4].
2   What light do these documents throw on the problems of the Privy Council in financing war in Elizabethan England?
3   Why do you suppose that the Queen did not summarily dismiss all those local governors who refused to cooperate with her policy?
4   Can documents 5.1 to 5.5 be used to show the unpopularity of Elizabeth's war with Spain in the 1590s?

Although the powers of the Lord Lieutenant and his deputies were considerable, most administration was carried out by local gentlemen acting through commissions from central government. Of these commissions by far the most important was that of 'the peace', which was issued annually. During Elizabeth's reign the role of the Justices of the Peace expanded considerably, as her government increasingly left the implementation of laws in their hands:

5.6

The justices of peace be men elected out of the nobility, higher and lower, that is the dukes, marquises, barons, knights, esquires and gentlemen, and of such as be learned in the laws, such and in such number as the prince shall think meet, and in whom for wisdom and discretion he putteth his trust, inhabitants within the country; saving   5
that some of the high nobility and chief magistrates for honour's sake are put in all or in the most of the commissions of all the shires of England . . .
The justices of the peace be those in whom at this time for the repression of robbers, thieves and vagabonds, of privy complots and   10
conspiracies, of riots and violences, and all other misdemeanours in

the commonwealth the prince putteth his special trust. Each of them hath authority upon complaint to him of any theft, robbery, manslaughter, murder, violence, complots, riots, unlawful games, or any such disturbance of the peace and quiet of the realm, to commit   15
the persons whom he supposeth offenders to the prison . . . till he and his fellows do meet . . . These do meet four times in the year, that is, in each quarter once . . .

The justices of the peace do meet also at other times by commandment of the prince upon suspicion of war, to take order for   20
the safety of the shire, sometimes to take musters of harness and able men, and sometimes to take order for the excessive wages of servants and labourers, for excess of apparel, for unlawful games, for conventicles and evil orders in alehouses and taverns, for punishment of idle and vagabond persons.

Sir Thomas Smith, *De Republica Anglorum*, pp. 85–8

Not everyone was satisfied with the work of the Justices of the Peace, as can be seen in this parliamentary speech of 1601:

5.7

Mr Glascock spoke and said: . . . A Justice of Peace is a Living Creature, that for half a dozen of Chickens will Dispense with a whole Dozen of Penal Statutes: We search and Ingross; they retail. These be the Basket-Justices, of whom the tale may be justified, of a Justice whom I know, to whom one of his Poor Neighbours coming,   5
said: Sir, I am very highly rated in the Subsidy Book; I do beseech you to help me. To whom he answered, I know thee not. Not me? (quoth the Countryman) Why, your Worship had my Team and mine oxen such a day; and I have been ever at Your Worship's service; Have you so? (quoth the Justice) I never remember I had any such   10
matter; not so much as a sheep's tail. So unless you offer sacrifice unto these Idol-Justices, of Sheep and Oxen, they know you not.

Mr Glascock to the House of Commons, 1601, from H. Townshend, *Historical Collections*, 1680, pp. 267–9

Questions

1   Comment on the following phrases in document **5.6**:
    (i) 'men elected out of the nobility' **[line 1]**
    (ii) 'excess of apparel' **[line 23]**.

2   What qualified those listed by Thomas Smith [5.6] to serve as
      Justices?
3   Does your wider reading lead you to accept the charges against the
      system of local government brought by Mr Glascock [5.7]?

The latter part of Elizabeth's reign witnessed an upsurge in social unrest
and local authorities joined central government in attempting to deal with
the problems of the poor. Unemployment and vagabondage were closely
linked but few contemporaries were able to see them as a result of rising
population. William Lambarde gives this account of the condition of the
Elizabethan poor:

5.8

The poor are exceedingly much multiplied because for the most part
all the whole children and brood of the poor be poor also, seeing that
they are not taken from their wandering parents and brought up to
honest labour for their living, but, following their idle steps . . . as
they be born and brought up, so do they live and die, most shameless   5
and shameful rogues and beggars.

And to the increase of these evils we have, as I said, a sort of poor
lately crept in amongst us and not before known to our elders: I
mean poor soldiers . . . There were always poor leprous, poor
lazarous, aged poor, sick poor, poor widows, poor orphans and such   10
like, but poor soldiers were either rarely or never heard of till now of
late. And this is the reason: not only in old time but within the reach
of our own memories . . . the nobility, knighthood and gentry of the
realm carried to the wars with them their freehold or copyhold
tenants, their able and wealthy neighbours, and their own menial and   15
household servants, of which three sorts two were able at their return
to live of their own, and the third was never forsaken of their lords
and masters under whom they had adventured. But now, when not
only our gaols are scoured and our highways swept but also the
cannels of our streets be raked for soldiers, what marvel is it if after   20
their return from the wars they do either lead their lives in begging
or end them by hanging. Nevertheless, we are by many duties most
bounden to help and relieve them, considering that they fight for the
truth of God and defence of their country; yea, they fight our own
war and do serve in our places, enduring cold and hunger when we   25
live at ease and fare well, lying in the open field when we are lodged

in our beds of down, and meeting with broken heads and limbs when we find it good and safe sleeping in a whole skin.

William Lambarde and Local Government, 1594, ed. C. Read, Folger Shakespeare Library, pp. 182–4

Contemporaries recognised the scale of the problem – by 1600 one in ten of the population was in need of regular relief and perhaps one in three in need of more occasional relief – but they did not properly understand its causes. These were largely the growth of population in a relatively rigid economy: more hands seeking work and more mouths seeking food pushed wages down and food prices (and other prices) up. The Queen, both Houses of Parliament, and local authorities joined together to find solutions to the problem. One early attempted solution was the Statute of Artificers of 1563:

5.9

Every person between the ages of twelve years and the age of three score years, not being lawfully retained, nor apprentice . . . nor being a gentleman born, nor being a student or scholar in any of the universities or in any school, nor having lands, tenements, rents or hereditaments of the clear yearly value of forty shillings for term of   5
life . . . shall after the foresaid last day of September now next ensuing by virtue of this statute, be compelled to be retained to serve in husbandry by the year, with any person that keepeth husbandry, and will require any such person so to serve within the same shire where he shall be so required.

Statute of Artificers 1563, in *Statutes of the Realm,* **vol. 4, p. 415**

As the reign progressed, legislation was developed which attempted both to assist the 'needy' poor and to punish idle rogues and vagabonds. In 1567, Thomas Harman described the many forms of vagabonds one might meet on an Elizabethan road:

5.10

Rufflers: sturdy vagabonds who begged from the strong and robbed the weak.

Upright men: vagabonds who were strong enough to be rulers among their fellows.

Hookers or Anglers: thieves who stole clothing etc. out of open windows by means of a hooked stick.

Wild Rogues: rogues born on the road of vagabond parents.

Pryggers of Prancers: horse stealers.

Palliards: beggars who exhibited artificial sores.

Abraham Men: beggars who pretended to be mad.

Counterfeit Cranks: beggars who pretended to have the falling sickness.

Dommerers: sham deaf-mutes.

Bawdy Baskets; female pedlars.

'Caveat for Common Cursetors', 1567, in *Tudor Economic Documents,* **ed. R. H. Tawney and E. Power, 1924, vol. 3, p. 407**

The following are certificates of beggars arrested by the first watchman at Southcley, Nottinghamshire in 1571:

5.11

A calendar of all the vagabonds, rogues and mighty valiant [= hardy] beggars taken there the first watch held the 20 August 1571, brought and examined before me, Nicholas Powtrell.

1   Joanne Holmes taken at Normanton as a valiant beggar, examined before me and whipped, punished and stocked, and sent from constable to constable the direct way to Faresley in the county of Warwick, where she last dwelled by the space of three years and more together.

2   Isabell Cotton, Anne Draper and John Draper taken at Normanton as vagrant persons, examined, whipped and punished, and after sent from constable to constable the direct way to Bolton in Lancashire, where they were born and dwell.

'Calendar of vagabonds . . .', 1571, in *Calendar of State Papers Domestic,* **Elizabeth, vol. 80, no. 27**

The large number of soldiers pressed for service in the last decade of Elizabeth's reign presented further problems. By 1597 Parliament was

determined to take vigorous action to suppress 'sturdy beggars', many of
whom were deserters, injured or maimed soldiers:

5.12

I   It shall and may be lawful . . . for the Justices of Peace of any
county or city in this realm . . . assembled at any Quarter Sessions[1]
. . . to erect . . . one or more Houses of Correction within their
several counties or cities . . .

II   And be it also further enacted by the authority aforesaid[2], that   5
all persons calling themselves scholars going about begging, all
seafaring men pretending [= claiming] losses to their ships or goods
on the sea going about the country begging, all idle persons going
about in any country either begging or using any subtle [= abtruse]
craft or unlawful games and plays, or feigning themselves to have   10
knowledge in physiognomy[3], palmestry[4] or other like crafty
[= cunning] science, or pretending that they can tell destinies,
fortunes or such other like fantastical imaginations, all persons that be
or utter themselves to be proctors[5], procurers [= agents], patent
gatherers or collectors for gaols, prisons or hospitals . . . shall be   15
taken, adjudged and deemed rogues, vagabonds and sturdy beggars,
and they shall sustain such pain and punishment as by this Act is in
that behalf appointed.

III   Every rogue, vagabond or sturdy beggar which shall be . . .
taken begging vagrant, wandering or misordering themselves in any   20
part of this realm . . . shall upon their apprehension by the
appointment of any Justice of the Peace . . . be stripped naked from
the middle upwards and shall be openly [= publicly] whipped until
his or her body be bloody . . . After which whipping the same person
shall have a testimonial . . . mentioning the day and place of his   25
punishment and the place whereto such person is limited to go, and
by what time the said person is limited to pass thither at his peril.

¹ 'Quarter Sessions' = county courts held four times a year
² 'the authority aforesaid' = that of Queen and Parliament
³ 'physiognomy' = divining of character and fate by an examination of facial
features
⁴ 'palmestry' = reading of palms
⁵ 'proctors' = collectors of alms

**Act for Punishment of Rogues, Vagabonds and Sturdy Beggars, 1597,
in *Statutes of the Realm*, vol. 4, part 2, p. 899**

Questions

1 What light do documents **5.8** to **5.12** throw on the nature, extent, and causes of vagrancy in Tudor England?
2 How practical do you suppose the Statute of Artificers [**5.9**] was as a solution to the problems outlined in **5.8**?
3 Why do you think that it was thought appropriate to deal with Joanne Holmes and other beggars as described in **5.11**?
4 How might those responsible for the 1597 statute [**5.12**] have defended its provisions?

But there was a humane side to the laws too, with a compulsory poor rate being levied on all householders from 1572. The new system was administered by parish officials but superintended by the Justices of the Peace, who in turn were answerable to the Privy Council.

Some of the larger towns anticipated government action, introducing their own programmes of poor relief and providing work for paupers. After 1576, Justices of the Peace were made responsible for finding materials for this work. However, in many cases the poor were already too weak and too ill to draw much benefit. In the next extract there are examples of poor relief given in Ipswich:

5.13

Richard Sexten admitted into Christ's Hospital the thirteenth day of June 1579 by Mr Gooding, one of the governors, and there to have a bed and room until further order be taken. His age 56. Born in Lancashire. Richard Sexten was admitted into the foundation the second day of January 1580, and to begin his relief of eight pence the   5
week the eighth day of the same month . . . This Richard Sexten put out of the foundation the 20 August 1583 by Mr Cutler, Mr Blowse, Mr Barker and Mr Martin, for whoredom, as he was charged withal, and put into an almshouse called the Pountnye, having his bed of flocks with the transom[1], his pair of blankets, two old coverlets, two   10
pairs of sheets, all his apparel [=clothes] saving the letters cut out which were on his gown at the commandment of Mr Bailiff Crane and the rest of the wardens.

[1] 'bed of flocks with the transom' = bed made of coarse tufts of wool or cotton, with a bolster

J. Webb (ed.), *Poor relief in Elizabethan Ipswich*, Suffolk Record Society, 1966, vol. 9, p. 97

There was a growing realisation that moral issues were at stake in the reformation of the poor. Towards the end of Elizabeth's reign, a large number of bills were passed in Parliament regulating the behaviour and manners of the poor. The act of 1597 was in itself a major step in the creation of a national system of poor relief:

5.14

1   Be it enacted . . . that the churchwardens of every parish, and four substantial householders there being subsidy men[1] . . . shall be called overseers of the poor of the same parish. And they . . . shall take order . . . with the consent of two or more such Justices of Peace, for setting to work of the children of all such whose parents 5 shall not be thought able to keep and maintain their children, and also such persons married or unmarried as, having no means to maintain them, use no ordinary and daily trade of life to get their living by. And also to raise weekly or otherwise (by taxation of every inhabitant and every occupier of lands in the said parish in such 10 competent [= sufficient] sum and sums of money as they shall think fit) a convenient stock of flax, hemp[2], wool, thread, iron and other necessary ware and stuff to set the poor on work, and also competent sums of money for and towards the necessary relief of the lame, impotent [= feeble], old, blind and such other among them being 15 poor and not able to work, and also for the putting out of such children to be apprentices . . .

4   . . . it shall be lawful . . . to bind any such children as aforesaid to be apprentices where they shall see convenient, till such man child shall come to the age of four and twenty years, and such woman child 20 to the age of one and twenty years . . .

7   . . . the parents or children of every poor, old, blind, lame and impotent person or other poor person not able to work, being of sufficient ability, shall at their own charges relieve and maintain every such poor person.

[1] 'subsidy men' = those sufficiently wealthy to pay parliamentary subsidies
[2] 'flax, hemp' = two different types of fibre

Act for the Relief of the Poor, 1597, in *Statutes of the Realm*, vol. 4, part 2, p. 896

Questions

1 How do documents **5.13** and **5.14** help to define 'the deserving poor'?
2 Are the provisions of the 1597 Act [**5.14**] an appropriate response to the problems of the poor?
3 Does **5.14** make you want to modify the answer you gave to Question 4, page 101?
4 Looking back over **5.8** to **5.14** as a whole, consider what considerations of fear and humaneness underpinned the Poor Laws.

6 Elizabeth's financial problems

Elizabeth inherited a difficult financial situation. Her sister Mary had left debts of £227,000, of which £106,000 was owed to the Antwerp Exchange at a high rate of 14 per cent. Moreover, any attempt to reduce these figures would have been hampered by expensive military commitments, both in Scotland and on the continent. Elizabeth herself was essentially conservative in matters of finance and believed in strict housekeeping. She and Cecil were able to use this approach to maintain the efficiency of the machine left to them by Mary's Treasurer, Winchester, but they were not willing to try to increase its efficiency. They managed to avoid national bankruptcy, which afflicted both France and Spain in this period, and in spite of the costs of later foreign wars, Elizabeth died only £350,000 in debt. However, the financial mechanism was outdated and proved an unfortunate legacy to her successors.

Throughout Elizabeth's reign, the government relied heavily on borrowing. At the outset Elizabeth benefited from the wise financial advice of Thomas Gresham:

6.1

It may please your Majesty to understand, that the first occasion of the fall of the exchange did grow by the King's Majesty, your late father, in abasing his coins from vi ounces fine to iii ounces fine. Whereupon the exchange fell from xxvi*s* viii*d* to xiii*s* iv*d* which was the occasion that all your fine gold was conveyed out of this your   5 realm.

Secondly, by the reason of his wars, the King's Majesty fell into great debts in Flanders. And for the payment thereof they had no other device but pay it by exchange, and to carry over his fine gold for the payment of the same.   10

Thirdly the great freedom of the Steelyard and granting of licence for the carrying of your wool and other commodities out of your realm, which is now one of the chief points that your Majesty hath to foresee in this your common weal; that you never restore the steads called the Steelyard again to their privilege, which hath been the   15

chief point in the undoing of this your realm, and the merchants of
the same . . .

. . . as the exchange is the thing that eats out all princes . . . if it be
not substantially looked into, so likewise the exchange is the chief and
richest thing only above all other, to restore your Majesty and your 20
realm to fine gold and silver, and is the mean that makes all foreign
commodities and your own commodities with all kind of victuals good
cheap, and likewise keeps your fine gold and silver within your realm
. . . and it please your Majesty to restore this your realm into such
state, as heretofore it hath been; first, your Highness hath no other 25
ways, but when time and opportunity serveth, to bring your base
money into fine of xi ounces fine, and so gold after the rate . . .

. . . to keep up your credit, and especially with your own merchants,
for it is they must stand by you at all events in your necessity.

Sir Thomas Gresham on the Fall of Exchanges, 1558, in J. Burgon,
Life and Times of Sir Thomas Gresham, 1839, vol. 1, pp. 483–6

Gresham wanted Elizabeth to prove her regime was credit-worthy, an
unusual quality among sixteenth-century governments. In 1571 he
advised her, 'Wishing that [he] were . . . able to persuade that payment
might be now made out of the subsidy money, which would not a little
advance her Majesty's credit among her own subjects if her Highness hereafter should have any occasion to borrow money'. Gresham was also
aware that the growth of the English money market was hampered by
restrictive legislation on the subject of usury. In 1560 he pressed Cecil to
remedy the situation, so that Elizabeth would be able to raise loans at home
rather than resort to Antwerp.

In 1569 Gresham told Cecil, 'I would wish that the Queen Majesty in this
time should not use any strangers but her own subjects whereby [the Duke
of Alva] and all other princes may see what a prince of power she is.'

It would appear that Cecil's own financial conservatism was at the root
of opposition to changes in the usury laws but Gresham continued to argue
that the Crown's own interests were being hampered by the prohibition of
interest, and in 1571 a new, more liberal law was passed:

6.2

Whereas in the parliament held the seven and thirty year of the reign
of our late sovereign lord King Henry the Eighth of famous memory,
there was then made and established one good Act for the

reformation of usury, by which Act the vice of usury was well
repressed . . . and where since that time by one other Act made in   5
the fifth and sixth years of the reign of our late sovereign lord King
Edward the Sixth the said former Act was repealed, and new
provisoes for repressing of usury devised and enacted, which latter
Act has not done so much good as was hoped it should, but rather
the said vice of usury . . . has much more exceedingly abounded, to   10
the utter undoing of many gentlemen, merchants, occupiers and other
. . . Be it therefore enacted that the said latter statute . . . shall . . .
be utterly repealed . . . and that the said Act, made in the said seven
and thirty year of King Henry the Eighth . . . shall be revived . . .
And be it further enacted that all bonds, contracts and assurances,   15
collateral [= additional] or other, to be made for payment of any
principal[1] or money to be lent . . . or for any usury in lending . . .
upon which loan . . . there shall be reserved . . . above the rate of ten
pounds for the hundred for one year shall be utterly void.

[1] 'principal' = capital sum

Act against Usury, 1571, in *Statutes of the Realm*, vol. 4, p. 542

Elizabeth's strict housekeeping meant that, by 1574, she was free from
debt for the first time. In addressing Parliament two years later, Sir Walter
Mildmay explained the significance of this achievement. The Queen had
inherited a realm, 'miserably overwhelmed with Popery, dangerously
afflicted with War, and grievously afflicted with Debts; the burden of which
three cannot be remembered without grief'. However, things were
different now:

6.3

Her Majesty hath most carefully delivered this Kingdom from a great
and weighty Debt, wherewith it hath long been burdened. A Debt
begun four years at the least before the death of King Henry the
Eighth, and not cleared until within these two years, and all that
while running upon Interest, a course able to eat up not only private   5
men and their patrimonies, but also Princes, and their Estates; but
such hath been the care of this time, as Her Majesty and the State is
clearly freed from the eating corrosive, the truth whereof may be
testified by the Citizens of London, whose bonds under the common
Seal of the City of assurance of payment being usually given and   10
renewed, and which have hanged so many years to their great danger,

and to the peril of the whole traffic are now all discharged, cancelled and delivered into the Chamber of London to their own hands. By means whereof the realm is not only acquitted of this great burden, and the Merchants free, but also her Majesty's credit thereby both at 15 home and abroad greater than any other Prince for money, if she need have, and so in reason it ought to be, for that she hath kept promise to all men, wherein other Princes have often failed to the hindrance of many.

Sir Walter Mildmay to the House of Commons, 1576, in Sir Simonds D'Ewes, *Journals of all the Parliaments During the Reign of Queen Elizabeth,* **1682, pp. 244–6**

Questions

1   What do you understand by the following phrases:
   (i) 'the steads called the Steelyard' [**6.1, lines 14–15**]
   (ii) 'that eats out all princes' [**6.1, line 18**]
   (iii) 'which have hanged so many years to their great danger' [**6.3, line 11**]?
2   What does Sir Thomas Gresham see as the cause of England's poor financial condition [**6.1**]?
3   From the evidence of documents **6.1** to **6.3**, how would a change in the country's usury laws allow Elizabeth to improve her credit [**6.1** to **6.3**]?

Elizabeth continued to raise loans at home, particularly towards the end of her reign when financial pressure became more severe. Through careful housekeeping, a cash surplus of over £300,000 had accumulated in the Exchequer by 1584, but the outbreak of war with Spain saw it dwindle away, forcing her to borrow heavily again.

   The lack of basic financial reforms began to have serious effects. Clearly both the Queen and the Lord Treasurer were opposed to the idea of raising taxation, for fear of alienating merchants and gentlemen on whom the government depended for support. Yet the crises of the second half of her reign forced Elizabeth to increase financial demands on Parliament. On two occasions Sir Walter Mildmay, when introducing the question of subsidies, explained the Queen's options to the assembled members:

6.4

   (a)   [The Queen] . . . cannot have without great inconvenience, those helps which in times of her Father, her Brother and Sister were used, as the abasing of Coin, which brought infinite sums to them, but wrought great damage to the Realm . . . the sale of Lands whereof came also very great sums of money, but that is not hereafter to be used, saving that by the same the Revenues of the Crown are greatly diminished, which it cannot more bear, the borrowing of money upon Interest the burden whereof the Realm hath felt so heavy as that is never more to be done, if by any means it may be avoided.

(b)   But lest that peradventure some may judge that the Contribution granted by us now five years past . . . might suffice for many years without any new; I dare assure you for the acquaintance that I have . . . with those her Majesty's Affairs, that the same hath not been sufficient to answer the extraordinary charges happened since then, especially those of Ireland, by the one half, but her Majesty hath supplied the rest out of her own Revenues sparing from her self to serve the necessity of the Realm, and shunning thereby Loans upon interest as a most pestilent Cancer that is able to devour even the States of Princes.

Sir Walter Mildmay to the House of Commons, (a) 1571, (b) 1576, from Sir Simonds D'Ewes, *Journals of all the Parliaments During the Reign of Queen Elizabeth*, 1682, p. 287

Parliamentary grants took two distinct forms: fifteenths and tenths, raising about £30,000; and a subsidy, raising somewhat less than £100,000. In the absence of efficient and paid bureaucrats, this money was collected by the local gentry, who assessed their own contributions. The problem was that, in spite of inflation and the escalating burden of foreign wars, the customary figure was assessed each time. Moreover, as the assessors were members of the gentry, they valued their own contributions as proportionately less of their income than those of the poorer groups:

6.5

21 July 1589. Letters sent unto the commissioners appointed for the assessment of the subsidies within the several counties of Somerset [and 32 others] . . . which were delivered to be dispersed accordingly

by John Unett, one of the messengers of her Majesty's Chamber . . .
Yet, considering the notable and evident abasing and diminution of 5
many men's values heretofore in their assessments under all
reasonable proportions, specially of men of the better state of
livelihood and countenance, and therewith also in many shires and
divisions such negligence, or in some parts appearance of corruption
for private gain, that was used in choice of the head collectors, as in 10
many places of the realm the collectors did not answer[1] their
collections at the times appointed by the space of many years, until
they were thereto forced by sundry processes. And some have not as
yet answered any part thereof, and some others have in their excuse,
being committed to prison, alleged that their masters by whom they 15
were named had part of their collection in their own hands, and some
others have been named of so mean livings, contrary to the statutes,
as there has been no means to recover off them their debts.

[1] 'answer' = account for

Acts of the Privy Council, 1589, vol. 17, pp. 413–15

The discussions which took place in Parliament in 1593 were the early
stages of the confrontation between Crown and Parliament over the issue
of financial control:

6.6

Sir Robert Cecil . . . showed unto the committees of this House the
great and present need of provision of treasure to be employed for
the defence of the realm against the invasion of the great and mighty
enemies unto this realm and State; and showing further, that the
double subsidy and Fifteenths and Tenths lastly granted unto her 5
Majesty, amounting but unto two hundred and four score thousand
pounds, her Majesty has nevertheless in these defensive wars
expended of her own treasure alone ten hundred and thirty thousand
pounds since the time of the granting of the said double subsidy . . .
To which he alleged that the usual late subsidies were very small and 10
were also imposted [= charged] for the most part upon the meaner
[= poorer] sort of her Majesty's subjects, declaring, that he knew one
shire of this realm wherein there were many men of good living and
countenance, but none of them in the said last subsidies assessed at
above four score pounds land per annum. And that in the city of 15

London also, where the greatest part of the riches of the realm are, there was no one assessed at above two hundred pounds goods a man . . .

Sir Walter Raleigh answered . . . They of Newcastle lie still for fear, because Bordeaux fleet was taken this year by the enemy. For the   20
enemy approaching us, and being our neighbour, as he is gotten to be, our trades will decay every day, and so our poverty increases every day more and more. And this is most certain, the longer we defer aid, the less able shall we be to yield aid. . . . So, in conclusion he agreed to three subsidies; in them the three pound man be spared,   25
and the sum that came from them be levied upon those of ten pounds and upwards . . .

Sir Francis Drake described the King of Spain's strength and cruelty where he came, and wished a frank [= unconditional] aid to be yielded to withstand him; and he agreed to three subsidies.   30

Sergeant Harris moved for three subsidies, but the ancient custom of payment to be retained; besides, no three pound men to be excused, for then every man will labour by his friend to be set [= charged] three pound.

Sir John Fortescue thought it liberal to grant three subsidies, but did   35
assure of his proper knowledge that three subsidies would not defray her Majesty's charges, though all other customs and revenues were added unto them . . .

Mr Heale . . . argued the wealth of the country to be greater than ever it was, affirming that of his knowledge from the Mount to   40
London the country was richer many thousand pounds than heretofore. He also urged the necessity, which being so great, and her Majesty having expended as was said since 'eighty eight above ten hundred and thirty four thousand pounds, and that only in Normandy, Brittany and in the Low Countries, and upon her navy   45
and artillery . . .' He thought more subsidies would be yielded; and if subsidies only, the richer men must be the more deeply charged, and the commissioners may have authority to force men.

Mr Francis Bacon assented to three subsidies, but not to the payments under six years. And to this propounded three questions.   50
The first, impossibility or difficulty; the second, danger or discontentment; and thirdly, a better manner of supply than subsidy.

For impossibility: the poor men's rent is such that they are not able
to yield it, nor to pay so much for the present. The gentlemen must
sell their plate, and farmers their brass pots, ere this will be paid. 55
And for us we are here to search the wounds of the realm and not to
skin them over: therefore not to persuade ourselves of their wealth
more than it is. The dangers are these. We shall first breed
discontentment in paying these subsidies, and in the cause endanger
her Majesty's safety, which must consist more in the love of the 60
people than in their wealth; and therefore not to give them
discontentment in paying these subsidies; thus we run into a double
peril . . .

Sir Thomas Heneage, her Majesty's Vicechamberlain, said . . . a
people sound in religion and faithful to the Queen and State were 65
never found to love their Prince so little as to be discontented. The
necessity of the time is to be considered.

**Debate in the House of Commons on the Subsidies, March 1593, in
Sir Simonds D'Ewes, *Journals of All the Parliaments During the
Reign of Queen Elizabeth*, pp. 483–96**

Questions

1   What light do documents **6.4** to **6.6** throw on the extent of the
     Crown's dependence on parliamentary supply?
2   What light do **6.4** to **6.6** throw on the weakness of the existing system
     of taxation?
3   Are there any difficulties for the historian in using these documents
     to give an accurate account of the state of Elizabethan finance?
4   Do you think that a general unwillingness to pay taxes weakened the
     war effort against Spain?

Finance was the key to Elizabeth's military strategy. She saw her ability to
remain solvent as the decisive weapon against Spain. However, poor
harvests in the 1590s reduced government income from regular sources
and Elizabeth was forced to borrow more from financiers like Palavicino.
The effects of rebellion in Ireland and the irresponsible administration of
the Earl of Essex are reflected in this extract from the budget for 1600:

6.7 (a)

Estimate of Her Majesty's domestic and foreign expenditure (1600) in £

The Privy Purse	2000
Band of Pensioners	4000
Treasurer of the Chamber	8000
Master of the Wardrobe	4000
Cofferer of the Household	4000
Master of the Jewelhouse	2000
Master of the Posts	2840
Ambassadors etc	4000
Officers of the Works	5000
Treasurer of the Navy	2000
Victualling of the Navy	15000
Lieutenant of the Ordnance	6000
Master of the Armoury	400
Lieutenant of the Tower	2000
Castles etc	4000
Justices' diets	1600
Ireland	320000
Low Countries	25000
Fees and annuities	26000
Total	459840

6.7(b)

Estimate of Her Majesty's yearly revenues of the Exchequer (1600) in £

Issues of Sheriffs	10000
Receivers of her Majesty's Possessions	60000
The Hanaper	4000
Alienations	4000
Customs and subsidies of ports	80000
Imposts of wine etc	24000
Licenses, Fines and casual	5000
Recusancy	7000
First Fruits and Tenths	20000
Subsidy of the Clergy	20000
Subsidy of the Laity	80000
Fifteenths and Tenths	60000
Total	374000

Calendar of State Papers Domestic, Elizabeth, 1600, vol. 276, fol. 99v

Questions

1   What do you understand by the following sources of revenue:
    (i) 'Issues of Sheriffs' [6.7b]
    (ii) 'The Hanaper' [6.7b]
    (iii) 'Alienations [6.7b]
    (iv) 'First Fruits and Tenths' [6.7b]?
2   Which of the revenue figures do you feel to be particularly low and
    why [6.7b]?

Revenue from customs dues was always at the mercy of international
relations and from 1568 onwards deteriorating relations with Spain
affected English trade in Europe. The decline of Antwerp produced an
intense struggle between the Merchants Adventurers and those who
opposed their monopoly and favoured an extension of free trade. Private
merchants wished to sell their cloth freely in Europe, without concentrat-
ing at Middleburgh and Emden, the Merchants Adventurers' ports. In
1587 Burghley wrote to Hatton, the Lord Chancellor, supporting a
suspension of the trade monopoly:

6.8

This great matter of the lack of vent, not only of clothes, which
presently is the greatest, but of all other English commodities which
are restrained from Spain, Portugal, Barbary, France, Flanders,
Hamburg and the States, cannot but in process of time work a great
change and dangerous issue [= result] to the people of the realm who   5
heretofore, in time of outward peace, lived thereby, and without it
must either perish for want, or fall into violence to feed and fill their
lewd appetites with open spoils of others, which is the fruit of
rebellion . . . The original cause is apparently the contentions and
enmities between the King of Spain and his countries, and her   10
Majesty and her countries. The reduction hereof to amity between
the princes, and to open traffic according to the ancient treaties of
intercourse, would be the sovereign[1] remedy . . . To have vent
increase, there must be more buyers and shippers than there are, and
seeing our merchants say that they cannot have sales sufficient . . .   15

1   It were good that the steelyard men were licensed to trade as they
were wont to do, with condition upon good bonds that our merchants
adventurers shall have their former liberties at Hamburg.

2   These steelyard merchants must also have a dispensation to
carry a competent [=sufficient] number of unwrought cloths that   20
are coarse, which are the cloths whereof the great stay[2] is in the
realm . . .

4   And if her Majesty . . . would abate [=deduct] only 2*s* upon a
cloth, I think there would grow no loss to her Majesty, having
respect to the multitude of the cloths that should be carried . . .   25

5   The strangers also must have liberty to buy in Blackwell Hall, or
else there may be a staple[3] set up in Westminster, out of the liberties
of the city of London, which, rather than London would suffer, I
think they will grant liberty to strangers in respect to the hallage
money[4] which they shall lease. Notwithstanding all these shows of   30
remedies, I could wish that our merchant adventurers were made
acquainted herewith, and to be warned that if they shall not amend
the prices to clothiers for their coarse cloth, whereby the clothiers
may be reasonably apparent gainers, and that to be put in practice
this next week, that then her Majesty will give authority to put the   35
former helps in practice.

[1] 'sovereign' = most effective
[2] 'stay' = lack of production
[3] 'staple' = storehouse or depot for provisions
[4] 'hallage money' = fee paid for goods sold in a market

**Burghley to Hatton, 12 May 1587, in Sir H. Nicholas, *Memoirs of Sir
Christopher Hatton*, pp. 470–2**

Questions

1   What do you understand by the following:
      (i) 'the lack of vent' **[6.8, line 1]**
      (ii) 'with open spoils of others' **[6.8, line 8]**?
2   What economic problems does Burghley attribute to the monopoly of
      the Merchants Adventurers?
3   Who were the 'strangers' **[line 28]**? What measures does Burghley
      suggest should be used in their favour?
4   Would it help our interpretation of this evidence to know that
      Burghley referred, earlier in the letter, to being in great pain while
      writing it?

The inflation of the sixteenth and seventeenth centuries was a general
pan-European phenomenon. From the 1550s contemporary writers were

noting its effects, although the reason for it eluded them. Until the 1570s, Tudor economists struggled with the fact that prices rose not only when food became scarce, but also when the supply of goods remained stable and the circulating medium increased. In their confusion they used the term 'dearth' both for food shortages and rising prices.

Commentators blamed inflation on the debasement of the coinage which had taken place under the early Tudors, particularly under Henry VIII. At the start of Elizabeth's reign, both William Cecil and Sir Thomas Smith advised the Queen to revalue the coinage: 'it was the honour of her Crown and the true wealth of herself and people to reduce the standard to the ancient parity and purity of her great-grandfather Edward IV.' According to Cecil, 'that realm cannot be rich whose coinage is poor or base'. Elizabeth ordered the debased money to be called in and replaced by new coinage. In the following memorandum we can see the reasoning behind the operation:

6.9

Her Highness weighing and considering the state of this her realm and crown in time past, the great expenses of her ancestors by reason of their wars, and their ability not only to support the same, but also to leave great treasure behind them; and conferring [=comparing] therewith all her long and happy peace . . . and the great want and   5
insufficiency of her revenues and treasures to supply the ordinary charge and defence of her dominions; she could not but with great care study thereupon, and devise for remedy of the same. She is . . . induced to conceive that the greatest and almost only cause thereof has proceeded by the enhancements of the coin in the time of her   10
father and brother, and that the only remedy thereof is to reduce the monies to the ancient standard of 3s 4d the ounce, as it was in the time of her said father . . .

1   . . . as for tenants of improved [=increased] rents, her Majesty is persuaded that it were not injurious if it should be enacted by   15
authority of her estates [=Parliament], that the tenant during his term from date of her proclamation should not answer [=pay] his lord's rent, but after the rate of the abatement [=reduction] of the value of the money, viz. for every pound a mark, where the lord shall not be much hindered, being able to perform almost every way as   20
much with the mark as he was with the pound.

2   For such as are in debt, if her Highness by consent of Parliament

shall provide that every man after the day of proclamation shall
accept his debt and payment according to the proportion of the
money reduced, viz. for every pound a mark, she thinks the creditor   25
not hindered . . .

4   . . . as concerning . . . the fear of transporting the treasure, being
fine [= pure], and in value as is here mentioned, it appears not unto
her Majesty how her merchant may more avail himself [= prosper]
than he does at this present, for the stranger [= foreigner] never   30
respects our value, but the goodness of our coin, be it gold or silver,
according to the richness and substance of his own, and so bargains
accordingly.

**Memorandum on the reasons moving Queen Elizabeth to reform the
coinage, 1559, in *Calendar of State Papers Domestic*, Elizabeth, vol.
11, no. 6,**

It was assumed by the Council that the alteration of the coinage from base
money to fine silver would result in a reduction in prices. However, this did
not occur and prices began to rise even more. Sir Thomas Smith, in his
Discourse of the Common Weal, detected another possible explanation for
the inflation:

6.10

Knight: If this were the chiefest cause of the dearth . . . how comes
            it to pass . . . that the prices of all things fall not back to
            their old rate, whereas now long since our English coin (to
            the great honour of our noble Princess which now reigns)
            has been again thoroughly restored to his former purity and   5
            perfection?

Doctor: . . . the great store and plenty of treasure, which is walking
            in these parts of the world, far more in these our days than
            ever our forefathers have seen in times past. Who does not
            understand of the infinite sums of gold and silver, which   10
            are gathered from the Indies and other countries and so
            yearly transported to these coasts?

Sir Thomas Smith, *Discourse of the Common Weal*, 1571, pp. 186f

However, the bullion argument was not generally understood and people
tended to turn to things which seemed to be more concrete explanations,

like greed or the selfishness of monopolists. Although some were aware of the rapid growth in population, they had yet to see how this could have contributed to the price rises. In 1594, William Lambarde commented:

6.11

> That the number of our people is multiplied, it is both demonstrable to the eye and evident in reason, considering on the one side that nowadays not only young folks of all sorts but churchmen also of each degree do marry and multiply at liberty, which was not want to be, and on the other side that we have not, God be thanked, been   5
> touched with any extreme mortality, either by sword or sickness, that might abate the overgrown number of us. And if all, then each sort, and in them the poorer sort also, must needs be augmented.

William Lambarde and Local Government, 1594, ed. C. Read, p. 182

In 1601 Gerrard De Malynes suggested a way of controlling prices:

6.12

> Plenty of money makes generally things dear, and scarcity of money makes likewise generally things cheap. Whereas things particularly are also dear or goods cheap according to plenty or scarcity of the things themselves, or the use of them. According to the plenty or scarcity of the money then, generally things become dearer or goods cheap,   5
> whereunto the great store or abundance of money and bullion, which of late years is come from the West Indies into Christendom, has made everything dearer according to the increase of money, which has caused a great alteration and enhancing of the price of everything, and most especially because the money itself was altered in valuation   10
> in some countries.

Gerrard de Malynes, *A Treatise of the Canker of England's Common Weal*, 1601

Inflation meant that Elizabeth was unable to finance her government without resorting to Parliament for subsidies. This was to become a fundamental problem for her successors, though even before the end of her reign there were signs of developing opposition.

The large increase in prices harmed the poor most. The food price index, standing at 315 at the beginning of Elizabeth's reign, reached 530 by the end. Moreover, the purchasing power of an agricultural labourer's wages declined alarmingly and the four consecutive harvests from 1594 to 1597 were deficient. At Coventry in 1597 foodstuffs were 'so extreme dear that many good householders sold up all they had and were fain to beg.' Shakespeare's Titania gives a vivid picture of the suffering of the poor during the 1590s:

6.13

> The ox hath therefore stretch'd his yoke in vain,
> The ploughman lost his sweat, and the green corn
> Hath rotted 'ere his youth attain'd a beard:
> The fold stands empty in the drowned field,
> And crows are fatted with the murrion flock . . .   5
> No night is now with hymn or carol blest . . .
> the seasons alter: hoary-headed frosts
> Fall in the fresh lap of the crimson rose . . .
> . . . the spring, the summer,
> the childing autumn, angry winter, change   10
> Their wonted liveries, and the mazed world,
> By their increase, now knows not which is which.

W. Shakespeare, *A Midsummer Night's Dream*, Act 2, Scene 2

Questions

1   Who would lose out if recoinage was introduced [6.9]?
2   What is the meaning of the term 'dearth' as used by the Knight in document **6.10**?
3   In what ways are the observations contained in document **6.11** typical of the Elizabethan period?
4   Are the economic arguments used by Malynes [6.12] convincing from an Elizabethan viewpoint? What can the historian learn from them about the economic issues of the time?
5   How does Shakespeare convey the suffering of the ordinary folk in the 1590s [6.13]? How useful are these observations for the historian, compared with those of Lambarde [6.11]?
6   In view of the dates of documents **6.9** to **6.12** what does the historian gain from a comparison between these sources?

Bibliography

Source material

Useful source material can be found in the following books:

Cross, C, *The Royal Supremacy in the Elizabethan Church*, Allen and Unwin, 1969

Elton, G. R, (ed), *The Tudor Constitution*, 2nd edn. Cambridge University Press, 1982

Hurstfield, J. and Smith, A. G. R, (eds), *Elizabethan People*, St Martin's Press, 1972

Tawney, R. H. and Power, E, (eds), *Tudor Economic Documents*, 3 vols, Longman, 1924

General texts

For good general surveys the following are recommended:

Elton, G. R, *England under the Tudors*, 2nd edn, Methuen, 1974

Haigh, C, (ed), *The Reign of Elizabeth I*, Macmillan Problems in Focus, 1984

MacCaffrey, W. T, *The Shaping of the Elizabethan Regime*, Cape, 1969

MacCaffrey, W. T, *Queen Elizabeth and the Making of Policy 1572–1588*

Palliser, D. M, *The Age of Elizabeth 1547–1603*, Longman, 1983. Excellent survey of economic and social affairs

Rowse, A. L, *The England of Elizabeth*, Macmillan, 1950

Smith, A. G. R, *The Emergence of a Nation State 1529–1660*, Longman 1984

Williams, P, *The Tudor Regime*, Oxford, 1979

Biographies

Fraser, A, *Mary Queen of Scots*, Weidenfeld and Nicholson, 1969. A monumental biography on Mary Stuart

Hurstfield, J, *Elizabeth I and the Unity of England*, English Universities Press, 1960. Biographies on Elizabeth are numerous, but this one is particularly good

Johnson, P, *Elizabeth I, a Study in Power and Intellect*, Weidenfeld and Nicholson, 1974. Likewise a rewarding biography

Neale, J. E, *Queen Elizabeth*, Cape, 1934. Another very good biography

Neale, J. E, *Elizabeth I and her Parliaments*, 2 vols, Cape, 1953 and 1957. A significant book, whose views are being vigorously challenged

Read, C, *Mr Secretary Walsingham and the Policy of Queen Elizabeth*, 3 vols, Oxford, 1925. Great detail on Elizabethan government affairs. Likewise the two books listed below
Read, C, *Mr Secretary Cecil and Queen Elizabeth*, Cape, 1955
Read, C, *Lord Burghley and Queen Elizabeth*, Cape, 1960

The Settlement of 1559

Haugaard, W, *Elizabeth and the English Reformation*, Cambridge, 1968. A view of reactions to the Settlement
Hudson, W. S, *Cambridge and the Elizabethan Settlement of 1559*, Durham NC 1980
Jones, N. L, *Faith by Statute: Parliament and the Settlement of Religion 1559*, Royal Historical Society Studies in History, XXXII, 1982
Jones, N. L, 'Elizabeth's First Year' in C. Haigh, (ed), *The Reign of Elizabeth*, Macmillan Problems in Focus, pp. 27–53
Neale, J. E, *Elizabeth I and her Parliaments*, 2 vols, Cape, 1953 and 1957. Contrast this with the views of N. L. Jones and W. S. Hudson

Marriage, the Succession and foreign policy

The study of foreign policy from original sources involves consulting the State Papers of the Public Record Office in London, though other documents are kept at the British Museum, London, and at Hatfield House, Herts.
Doran, S, *England and Europe, 1485–1603*, Longman Seminar Studies in History, 1986
Fletcher, A, *Tudor Rebellions*, 2nd edn, Longman Seminar Studies in History, 1974. Includes a good survey of the Northern Revolt of 1569
Mattingly, G, *The Defeat of the Spanish Armada*, Cape, 1959. A scholarly and exciting account of events in Europe 1587–8
Ramsay, G. D, 'The Foreign Policy of Elizabeth I', in C. Haigh, (ed), *The Reign of Elizabeth I*, Macmillan Problems in Focus, pp. 147–68
Wernham, R. B, *Before the Armada: The Growth of English Foreign Policy 1485–1588*, Cape, 1966. Very useful
Wernham, R. B, *After the Armada: Elizabethan England and the Struggle for Western Europe, 1588–95*, Oxford, 1983. Very useful
Wilson, C, *Queen Elizabeth and the Revolt of the Netherlands*, University of California Press, 1970. Useful study

The Church of England and Puritanism

Alexander, H. G, *Religion in England, 1558–1662*, Hodder and Stoughton, 1968. A good general account.
Collinson, P, 'The Elizabethan Church and the New Religion', in C. Haigh, (ed), *The Reign of Elizabeth I*, Macmillan Problems in Focus, pp. 169–94
Collinson, P, *The Elizabethan Puritan Movement*, Cape, 1967
Collinson, P, *The Religion of Protestants*, Oxford University Press, 1982
Cross, C, *Church and People 1450–1660*, Fontana, 1976. A good general account.

Haigh, C, *Reformation and Resistance in Tudor Lancashire*, Cambridge University Press, 1975. An excellent local study

Haigh, C, 'Puritan Evangelism in the Reign of Elizabeth I', *English History Review*, vol. xcii, 1977, pp. 30–58. Another excellent study into the effect of the new religion on local communities

Knappen, M. M, *Tudor Puritanism*, University of Chicago Press, 1938

Lake, P, *Moderate Puritans and the Elizabethan Church*, Cambridge University Press, 1982

Manning, R. B, *Religion and Society in Elizabethan Sussex*, Leicester, 1969. Another very good local study

McGrath, P, *Papists and Puritans under Elizabeth I*, Blandford, 1967. Excellent book looking at the problem of nonconformity to the new Church, both Catholic and Protestant

Catholicism under Elizabeth

Bossy, J, *The English Catholic Community 1570–1850*, Darton, Longman and Todd, 1975

Dures, A, *English Catholicism, 1558–1642*, Longman Seminar Studies in History, 1983. A good survey of the main issues

Haigh, C, *Reformation and Resistance in Tudor Lancashire*, Cambridge University Press, 1975. An invaluable local study. See also R. B. Manning (section above)

Haigh, C, 'The Continuity of Catholicism in the English Reformation', *Past and Present*, vol. xciii, pp. 37–69; and 'From Monopoly to Minority: Catholicism in Early Modern England', *Transactions of the Royal Historical Society*, 1981, pp. 129–47, Essays.

Haigh, C, 'The Church of England, Catholics and the People' in C. Haigh, (ed), *The Reign of Elizabeth I*, Macmillan Problems in Focus, pp. 195–219

McGrath, P, *Papists and Puritans under Elizabeth I*, Blandford, 1967

Scarisbrick, J. J, *The Reformation and the English People*, Oxford University Press, 1984

Elizabeth and the local communities

Beier, A. L, *The Problem of the Poor in Tudor and Early Stuart England*, Methuen, 1983

Bindoff, S. T, 'The Making of the Statute of Artificers' in *Elizabethan Government and Society*, (eds), S. T. Bindoff et al, Athlone, 1961

Boynton, L. O. J, *The Elizabethan Militia*, Macmillan, 1967

Cruickshank, C. G, *Elizabeth's Army*, 2nd edn, Oxford University Press, 1966

Elton, G. R, *The Tudor Constitution*, 2nd edn, Cambridge University Press, 1982. A good survey of central and local government, also containing numerous documents

Gleason, J. H, *The Justices of the Peace in England 1558–1640*, Oxford University Press, 1969

Haigh, C, (ed), *The Reign of Elizabeth I*, Macmillan Problems in Focus, pp. 221–45

Leonard, E. M, *The Early History of English Poor Law*, Cambridge University Press, 1965

Slack, P. A, 'Vagrants and Vagrancy in England 1598–1664' *Economic History Review*, 1974, pp. 360–79.

Slack, P. A, 'Poverty and Social Regulation in Elizabethan England', in C. Haigh (ed), *The Reign of Elizabeth I*, Macmillan Problems in Focus, pp. 221–45

Smith, A. G. R, *The Government of Elizabethan England*, Arnold, 1967. A good, general account

Williams, P, *The Tudor Regime*, Clarendon Press, 1979. Another good, general account

Williams, P, 'The Crown and the Counties', in C. Haigh (ed), *The Reign of Elizabeth I*, Macmillan Problems in Focus, pp. 127–46

Elizabeth's financial problems

Alsop, J. D, 'Government, Finance and the Community of the Exchequer', in C. Haigh (ed), *The Reign of Elizabeth I*, Macmillan Problems in Focus, pp. 101–23

Alsop, J. D, 'The Theory and Practice of Tudor Taxation, *English History Review*, 1982, pp. 1–30

Dietz, F. C, *English Public Finance 1558–1641*, New York, 1932. Though dated, still a recommendable book

Hurstfield, J, 'The Profits of Fiscal Feudalism 1541–1602', *Economic History Review*, 1955–6, pp. 53–61

Miller, H, 'Subsidy Assessment of the Peerage in the Sixteenth Century', *Bulletin of the Institute of Historical Research*, 1955, pp. 15–34

Outhwaite, R. B, 'Royal Borrowing in the Reign of Elizabeth I: the Aftermath of Antwerp', *English History Review*, 1971. Very important essay

Outhwaite, R. B, *Inflation in Tudor and Early Stuart England*, Macmillan, 1969

Pallisser, D. M, *The Age of Elizabeth 1547–1603*, Longman, 1983

Williams, P, *The Tudor Regime*, Clarendon Press, 1979

Titles in the series:

Index